# Growing
# ORCHIDS
## Cymbidiums and Slippers

# Growing ORCHIDS

*Book One*
*Cymbidiums and Slippers*

J.N. Rentoul

TIMBER PRESS
Portland, Oregon

Published in North America by
Timber Press
9999 S.W. Wilshire
Portland, OR 97225

ISBN 0-88192-009-6 Cased
ISBN 0-88192-010-X Paper

First published in Australia 1980 by Lothian Publishing Company Pty Ltd
11 Munro Street, Port Melbourne, Victoria 3207

Printed in Hong Kong through Bookbuilders Ltd

# Contents

Paphio. callosum

Most people read books, but it would be interesting to know how many of them read introductions. Naturally, many of these are formalities. This one is different — it has a message. The plants you are about to grow or are growing have a history.

While it is possible to grow plants and be quite unmoved by their history, a smattering often helps in understanding them. In the years from about 1780 onward they have continued to interest people and have lost none of their power to attract. There are no mysterious qualities about them — they are simply a phase in evolution and along with all other things follow a pattern of development to conform to the environment of any period. The Australian orchids confirm this view by the way they have evolved to suit the sometimes harsh climatic changes of that country.

The appearance of orchids in British and European gardens was originally perhaps just by chance, because they were first imported to those countries as inclusions with other plants and trees sought for their rarity, novelty, beauty and perhaps strangeness.

The innovation of heating glass-houses through piped hot water brought a new era to exotic plant culture, replacing a system which served very well to grow some plants but which was a failure with orchids.

Privately sponsored plant collectors were sent to other countries to collect specimens, one of these sponsors being the Horticultural Society of Great Britain. It is not easy to visualise the great wealth of some of the private sponsors of this early period of orchid culture or the size of the establishments where they were cultivated.

Initially the plants were killed almost as fast as they were unpacked and housed. Many flowered before they died, further stimulating the interest and perhaps at times the cupidity, too, of the owners.

Dr John Lindley, Professor of Botany at University College, London, about the 1830 period, who had a lot to do with the classifying and naming of these new plants, wrote in a paper delivered at a session of the Horticultural Society: 'The time is not so distant when the beauty of the dendrobiums and bulbophyllums of India, of the oncidiums of the West Indies, of the aerides of China and of the epidendrums of Peru will add a charm to every hot-house.'

Hot-house was the correct term applicable, as the general thought was that as these plants came from tropical countries they must need intense heat to survive. They were literally cooked, first because of lack of understanding and second because the collectors who sent the plants did not indicate that so many of them grew at altitudes of some 1000 to 2000 metres in climates which, while not cold, were at least moderate. It has since become one of the primary lessons for all aspiring orchid growers.

The immense size of the orchid family of plants as a whole became known gradually over the 200-odd years following their initial cultivation in glass-houses and new members of the family are still being catalogued and named. It stands at the rough-and-ready figure of some 30 000 species in 1200-odd genera.

It is beyond the capability of one mind or one person to begin to understand this botanical colossus and the relationship which exists between its flowers and the insect world. A large number of people are constantly reclassifying, revising and correcting the relationships of its members, one to another. Most of this work is clearly voluntary, although some is sponsored by educational, government and privately funded trusts.

Even this immense species catalogue is dwarfed by the hybrid list, in which the cymbidium section, with some 9000 names, and the paphiopedilum section, with 13 000-odd, are but a part of the whole, which comprises more than 100 000 named hybrids. While many of these are no longer in cultivation, they represent cross-pollinations, seed-raising and flowering of plants, their registration and appreciation by someone.

It is all the 'someones' who make up the orchid-growing communities of all races, growing their plants in many different ways and in all climates.

It was for the 'someones' eventually that the first garden hybrid orchid, raised by James Dominy and named *Calanthe* Dominii, had a tremendous impact. He produced it in 1856 and Dr Lindley, when he saw it in James Veitch and Sons' nursery in England, said to James Dominy with perhaps prophetic vision, 'Why, you will drive the botanists mad!'

In the light of the 1970-80 decade and those preceding it, the achievement of James Dominy was as nothing compared with the complexities of the inter-generic hybrid list, which is quite sufficient to give many botanists cause for misgivings about several supposedly rock-bottom theories.

In spite of at least one supposed departure from the rectitude of a clean family line in Phaiocymbidium Chardwarense, the cymbidiums are totally inbred as a genus and the same may be said of the paphiopedilums. Each has its devotees and they are somewhat insular in cultivation. This book is chiefly about these two genera.

As species, both are under threat of extinction, perhaps more from depredation than climate or environmental changes although this aspect is hastened all the time by human need and human greed. In the short 200-year period of orchid cultivation since the 1780s to the writing of this book, so many changes have taken place. Even the countries where the plants were discovered have in many instances been renamed.

It is more or less the duty of orchid growers everywhere, as individuals and collectively, to use some of their time and money to maintain the life cycle of orchids in their native environments so far as is possible in a changing world. And this is the message: The power of thought is immense — think about it.

The illustrations for the book were taken with three cameras, most of them by the author and many of the color transparencies are of plants grown by him. In only a few instances was flash or artificial light used. Where necessary a Rollei 128 BC unit was used, at times augmented with a National slave unit for larger subjects. This unit was adaptable to all three cameras. However, most of the photography was in daylight, with exposure times of as low as half a second and apertures of f.16 or f.22. All cameras were single lens reflex models.

The 35-millimetre camera used was a Pentax Model S, a very old but reliable instrument with hand-set aperture and focusing. The light meter used suited the camera speeds very well and was a Yashica Yem-31 Super. The lens of the camera was the usual Takumar 2.2, 55-millimetre standard fitting and was used in conjunction with a 2-millimetre ring and number 1, 2 and 3 proxars matched to the lens.

The 60 x 60 millimetre square camera was a Praktisix-II, a rather heavy instrument but fitted with a very fine Carl Zeiss Biometar 2.8, 80-millimetre lens. This camera was used for some of the color pictures as well as the black and whites. It also was used with rings and proxars, the latter made by Canon but fitting the camera. The same light meter matched this camera.

The third camera was a Mamiya M645, comparatively new on the market at that time. In spite of its complexity it is a very fine camera to use, well balanced and light. The shutter of this camera proved faster than that of the other two, possibly indicating the electronic shutter's accuracy. Adjustment of one stop had to be made when using the Yashica light meter. The lens of the Mamiya was that fitted as standard, a Sekor 2.8, 80-millimetre type and a set of related rings gave an aperture automation not present on the other cameras. With a related hand-grip it proved a very easy camera to take either flash or natural light pictures down to 1/30th of a second.

The films used varied but were mostly Agfapan 100 ASA for black and white or Agfachrome 50 S for the larger color transparencies and Agfacolor 50 ASA for the 35-millimetre camera.

The pastel drawings are by Joan Skilbeck, granddaughter of the author. Most were copied from various books, some of which are long out of print. Although only young, the artist displays considerable natural talent.

*Cymbidium* Charmant
'Kurnbrook Glory' grown by
George Leverett.

# Part 1
## *Cymbidiums*

# The Cymbidium

Cymbidiums are the most popular cultivated orchids in many parts of the northern and southern hemispheres. To many people they are simply 'orchids', their generic name sometimes unknown to them.

These people describe the plant and it is unmistakable — a cymbidium; the name derived from a Greek word *kumbe* a boat, referring to a hollow recess in the labellum or lip, according to Johnson's Botanical Dictionary. Paxton's Dictionary from about 1850-60 gives the derivation as from the Greek word *kymbos,* a hollow recess. In the manual of orchid genera written by Richard Schultes and Arthur Pease the derivation is given as from the Greek word *kymbes,* a boat-shaped cup. The reference is to the boat-shaped lip or labellum, which is really the feature point of most cymbidium flowers.

Most orchid names have a Greek or Latin origin. The word 'cymbidium' should be more commonly used than it is.

These orchids belong to a genus of plants which grow in certain areas from Northern India in a broad arc through Asia to Australia, the southern end of the arc in New South Wales.

A 'genus' is a family of plants in which there are any number of members, known as 'species', a word which is spelt the same for one member or several. In turn, members of a species have characteristics which distinguish them and they are known as 'varieties'. These differences are morphological. 'Morphology' means a difference in size of the plant, shape of the leaves, size of flowers, but not necessarily color and other features, as compared with other varieties.

These words will occur throughout the book, are easy to understand and are the only ones correctly applicable.

Some cymbidiums and other orchids are known by more than one name. Such as *Cymbidium grandiflorum,* which is also known as *Cymbidium hookeranum.* The first name is the correct one and the other is known as a synonym which, if used, is given as *Cymbidium grandiflorum* (syn. *hookeranum*).

It is easy to go on from here expecting everyone to know what I am writing about.

There are more than sixty species of the genus cymbidium and hundreds of varieties. The names such as *Cymbidium grandiflorum* or *Cymbidium lowianum* and all the other species names were conferred by botanists who handled the material when first sent from the country of origin to Europe, Britain or other places.

It was examined and given a name which was registered at such places as Kew Gardens, England, or other herbariums throughout the world. At times the same material was sent to two or more herbariums and some confusion occurred, following which a priority was worked out as in the case of *Cymbidium grandiflorum.*

Cymbidiums gained their name in 1799 from Olaf Swartz, a Swedish botanist. In general conversation they are commonly referred to as cyms or cymbids.

The word 'clone' also appears in orchid literature. It signifies the total number of plants of a variety. A well known hybrid cymbidium variety is *Cymbidium* Mary Ann 'Simplicity'. No matter where in the world that cymbidium is grown it will be part of that clone.

Cymbidiums as we know them are beautiful, brilliant, long-lasting hybrid orchids. Where did they come from? How much more can they be developed? Will they always be grown as they now are, or will they go out of cultivation forsaken for something else? How can they be grown?

Some of those questions will be answered in the following chapters, some will remain unanswered.

Cymbidiums came from various parts of Indo-Asia and these were direct results of natural evolution; others as we know them today are the result of mankind's dissatisfaction with nature. In some eyes mankind has improved them, but only by breaking all the primary rules laid down by natural evolution.

In temperate climates cymbidiums are easier to grow than in other climates. But in cultivation over the years since about 1900 more cymbidium hybrids have been produced and discarded than possibly any other genus. Some 75 per cent of the hybrids produced have slipped out of sight, as a brief look through *Sanders Hybrid List* makes plain.

The plants look superficially like some which grow in the Australian bush. Like sword-grass, for instance, with its long curving leaves and close-set base.

The formation or morphology of the plant could best be likened to that of the iris family, where new growths appear each year and produce flower spikes. Each growth is separate and is really an extension of the plant on a tough interconnecting sub-surface system called a rhizome. It is from this rhizome that the roots emerge to penetrate the growing medium. As the plant ages the older parts die off, although still attached to the rhizome. First the leaves are cast, usually slowly over a couple of years, then the leaf bases die off.

However, in cymbidiums this older part of the plant acts like a storehouse for the leading portion, filling out in good conditions then sending the sap and vitality into the leading portions when hard times come. When the plant becomes too large or the growing material loses its ability to feed it, then a changeover and division becomes necessary.

In their brief history as cultivated garden plants, cymbidiums, whether grown under glass or other protective material or even in open rockeries or raised beds, are a reflection of their times. Originally grown as species, they were later subjects of artificial cross-pollination in the same way as various other genera of plants which preceded them.

Natural cross-pollination occurs in nature as species interrelate to produce new species, and botanists surmise that at least three or four new species of orchids appear each year in this way. But there is no way in which this can be related to the progress of cymbidiums in the years 1930 onward.

It does seem strange that as a genus they were so long in cultivation before they were hybridised, considering the numbers of hybrids in other genera before 1900. The areas where they originate, however inaccessible, were under domination and trade with European nations long before the Americas. Although vandas and dendrobiums and many other genera were common in early collections the cymbidiums were somehow neglected.

Several species were grown in the late 1800s, but apart from *Cymbidium grandiflorum, Cymbidium giganteum* and *Cymbidium eburneum,* the cymbidiums with most influence on our hybrids did not appear until the beginning of this century. In some ways this was natural, since the inclusion of the genus in orchid collections stimulated the search for other species and the further search for better varieties of those known. Curiosity probably motivated early hybridists, followed later by commercial exploitation of the primary results.

Considered in the light of techniques available to seed raisers in that period, compared with the high level of competence of the 1930-70 era, it is surprising that so many hybrids were created. But it should also be remembered that the hybridists of those times were skilful and lack of automation and facilities were compensated for by devotion and a conscientious attitude to the work. The working day was from daylight to dark and distractions few.

The eagerness for new material was also probably responsible for much of the attention given to the work. There was no such thing as the dull repetition of flasking and reflasking and replanting common to the process now, or many of the other tasks in the orchid nursery.

Most orchid growing and seed raising and the routine work in cultivating orchids were part of ordinary horticulture, and boys and men showing aptitude were soon moved into the specialist category full-time. Much of the history of this period is obtainable in volumes of *The Orchid Review,* which was founded in 1893, and down through the various periods through the publication of *The Orchid Album,* a complete set of which is now worth from $15 000 to $20 000, to Bateman's book *Orchids of Mexico and Guatemala,* recently reprinted in a limited edition.

It should be realised that all cymbidium hybridising is largely a hit-and-miss affair. It began that way and to a degree remains so. Predictions of characteristics of a particular cross-pollination are worth no more now than they were at inception of hybridising, although some colors may be forecast with a little more certainty than others.

The uncertainty is a component of the mixed-heritage hybrids such as *Cymbidium* Legaye (*Cymbidium* Stanley Fouraker x *Cymbidium* Rampur), to take a random selection, rather than of primary hybrids such as *Cymbidium* Lowio-Eburneum. *Cymbidium* Legaye could be white, cream, yellow, bronze, green or gold, but scarcely pink.

There are justifiable reservations about growing cymbidiums in the hotter, drier parts of Australia and the semi-tropical areas, but I have seen them growing and flowering as far north as Mackay, Queensland. Growing them requires some skill and considerable work over and above that for ordinary gardening, but although complaints are frequent about cutting lawns and weeding gardens, they are seldom heard about the work involved in growing orchids. And there is no place like a nice warm glass-house in winter in which to lurk and look at things.

The history of cymbidiums in Australia is recorded in the *Australian Orchid Review* and little other material or books. It commenced with importation from England, Europe and plant exporters in India, among whom was the Chandra nursery, owned by Pradhans, and another owned by people named Ghose.

A very early reference occurs in the *Gardeners' Chronicle* of 13 July 1901: 'Although crosses have long been known in Europe between *C. lowianum* and *C. eburneum,* in which both have figured as the seed bearing parent, the one which we illustrate . . . is the first, so far as our knowledge goes, of a cross raised and flowered in Australia. According to information kindly furnished by Messrs. Sander and Co., of St. Albans, the seed of artificially fertilised flowers was sown by Mr. Godwin, gardener to John Hay, Esq., of the Crow's Nest, North Sydney, in the month of July, 1896, and a plant of this sowing flowered in April of last year (1900). As Mr. Sander remarks, ''it is evident that the climate of Australia is favourable to the raising of orchids; and, in fact, in this particular instance a record is established in rapid growth.'' The flowers measured 5½ inches across, which is equal to standard size.'

Some of the modern seed-raisers with all their facilities would possibly have flowering plants no sooner than those raised by Mr Godwin.

Probably the largest single collection of orchids and exotic plants in Australia at any time up to the 1930 era was at Ripponlea, Victoria, in the glass-houses of the Nathan family. It was formed very early in the twentieth century.

There was a constant flow of orchids into collections in Australia all through the following thirty years, but it was not until the 1930 decade that some clear vision of the future of the genus began to emerge. Many growers in Sydney and a few scattered in other states of Australia and elsewhere who were in touch with developments in England in particular started to import much better looking cymbidiums than had been available up to that time.

One of the first imports to Australia of any significance was the Nicholas collection, which came from McBeans, England, in that period and was first housed, I believe, in Hawthorn, Victoria, and later in heated glass-houses at Sherbrooke, in the Dandenong Ranges, Victoria. It contained some fine cymbidiums for that period, two of the best of which were *Cymbidium* Profusion 'Violacea' and *Cymbidium* Burnham Beeches 'Betty Bolton'. *Cymbidium* Profusion was a deep red-purple and *Cymbidium* Burnham Beeches a creamy yellow. There were many other excellent hybrids in the collection. Over some years these cymbidiums were grown, flowered and propagated by a couple of expert growers and many years later the whole collection was broken up and sold when the property was passed over to a trust attached to a children's hospital. It contained many other fine orchids as well as the cymbidiums.

In New South Wales many orchid growers imported fine collections of cymbidiums, mostly from England. Some remarkable colors included deep cigar-brown clones as well as good reds and clear greens. For that period color was more important than shape, although if both features combined in the one flower fairly high prices were paid for propagations. A salutary lesson for today's cymbidium growers lies in the speed with which these cymbidiums were relegated almost to oblivion.

Hybrid orchids were not easy to buy, as reference to Jack Bissett's catalogue of the period shows. He was associated with one of the first commercial orchid nurseries and distribution projects in Australia and was widely known. He was later joined by many other commercial orchid growers throughout Australia. The hub of the craft at that time was Sydney, although one of the first societies formed was the Victorian Orchid Club. Jack Bissett listed twenty-eight hybrid cymbidiums in his 1938 catalogue.

Arthur Yates, a Sydney grower, was importing plants from England between the end of the First World War and 1930 and gives a very clear description in *The Orchid Review* (England) of that period of his methods of rehabilitating and acclimatising the plants after their journey of several weeks. He also described his cymbidiums, including enormous plants of *Cymbidium lowianum* and *Cymbidium* Lowio-Eburneum about 1.75 metres (6 feet) across.

Another Sydney grower, F. O. Hedger, found his inspiration to begin growing orchids in the collection at that time cultivated in the Sydney Botanic Gardens. He

Cymbidiums in black and white do not signify very much to buyers. Although this one is pink, they are obtainable in all colors except blue and black.

9

asked the curator where he could get similar plants and was referred to Pradhans, of Sikkim, India. Eventually his parcel arrived, containing dendrobiums, vandas, phaius, coelogynes, saccolabiums, aerides, cypripediums, cymbidiums and some phalaenopsis. The last named would seem to be incongruous inclusions looked at from the viewpoint of modern cultivators. But he also expressed what to me was a familiar feeling of joy when he unpacked his new-found treasures.

Pradhans of India listed twenty-one species cymbidiums in their catalogue of the same period, but no hybrids. They would accept orders and send the plants by parcel post in woven cane baskets, which took some five or six weeks in transit. The plants would in many instances be leafless on arrival, but quickly sent up new growths and flowered. There was a Customs inspection but no plant quarantine. If most of the growers who took delivery were anything like me they opened the woven basket on the footpath outside the General Post Office and looked over their new-gained imports.

In the years of the second world war the whole import system built up over many years came to an end, and it was really the end of many old customs related to orchid plant importing. They never returned when the war was over.

Perhaps this period is reflected in a letter from A. J. Keeling, British orchid growers, in July 1942, after some two years of war, to W. A. Wright, of Heidelberg, Victoria, a well-known orchid grower: 'We have often sent large consignments of orchids to Canada, also to Mr Bissett, in New South Wales ... but of course it is a difficult proposition shipping plants to your country now in view of the length of time they are cased up. Pre-war it took about six weeks for plants to be landed in Sydney, now it takes anything up to 10 or 15 weeks, which is far too long for plants to be packed.'

In the early days of the second world war Jack Bissett took delivery of many cases of plants shipped from England and I remember seeing one lot unpacked. They were some of the cymbidiums which were in a few years to acquire the name 'Westonbirts' because of their breeding from *Cymbidium* Alexanderi 'Westonbirt'. At the time the plants were unpacked they were clusters of pseudo-bulbs with only pale white new leaves about 8-10 centimetres (3-4 inches) high, as they had been on the way for many weeks. Most came through the crisis under stringent shading and quickly grew into strong plants.

That indicates the system largely operating then, compared with the quick air freighting which followed the end of the war. It is quite obvious that even the war, detestable as it was, carried some good for orchid growers because of the remarkable development of long-range aviation with load-carrying planes. I planned to some degree what I was going to do about orchids when involved in New Guinea during the war.

Many fine cymbidiums were sent to Australia and America from England and Europe when the war came. Nearly all those sent to Australia completely changed cymbidium growing and many of the hybrids and nearly all the species which until that time had occupied the benches in collections soon disappeared. Traces of them still appear, however, but rarely with the labels they once so proudly bore.

In turn these new cymbidiums were also superseded, among them one which set a pattern of price and a standard which remained for quite some time. It was *Cymbidium* Girrahween 'Enid', a pink, which every cymbidium grower aspired to own. It was the ultimate. Not only was it a magnificent grower, it also had the most unlikely breeding of *Cymbidium lowianum* x *Cymbidium* Flamenco, imported into Australia by Carrington Deane of Sydney. It was not the only clone bearing the name *Cymbidium* Girrahween which went to the top of the list. However, they have almost totally disappeared, which is in some ways regrettable, because at least *Cymbidium* Girrahween 'Enid' could still hold its head up in most company.

*Cymbidium* Pauwelsii (*Cymbidium lowianum* x *Cymbidium insigne*) and *Cymbidium* Ceres (*Cymbidium i'ansonii* x *Cymbidium insigne*) were among those in the first group which so disappeared, the former frequently having spikes up to 2 metres (6 feet) or so and with up to twenty-five and more flowers.

These two orchids formed the baseline of British breeding, together with further use of *Cymbidium* Pearl (*Cymbidium* Alexanderi x *Cymbidium grandiflorum*). The first two led to production of *Cymbidium* Remus (*Cymbidium* Regulus x *Cymbidium* Joyful) and *Cymbidium* Pearl 'Magnificum' to *Cymbidium* Rio Rita 'Radiant'.

Books could be written about hybridising in cymbidiums, but these five orchids referred to in the previous paragraphs are a large book in themselves.

Two distinct trends in cymbidium breeding followed, with the Americans concentrating on 'bigger, brighter and better' and the British and European hybridists following a color pattern they had commenced pre-war.

It followed, then, that Australian hybridists had the best of both worlds and have produced cymbidiums along lines of 'form and substance' and colors equal to those produced elsewhere. One of the Australian innovators, Wondabah Orchids, run by the Giles family, continues to produce cymbidiums which satisfy growers.

Preceding the commercial hybridists in Australia, there were several individuals who wasted a great amount of valuable time trying to hybridise cymbidiums that were totally or partially sterile, because they concentrated on external features without knowing their chromosome make-up. In the 1960-70 period, many other hybridists were at work in Australia with a series of compatible chromosome parents, including a large number stemming from *Cymbidium* Alexanderi 'Westonbirt', along lines which intersected and criss-crossed as outstanding breeding clones appeared. Although at one time it was the exception to produce an outstanding cymbidium from any one cross-pollination, the odds against it have shortened to the extent where flowers to conform to standards can be produced almost at will and in a good percentage of any cross-pollination. Australia supplied many other countries eventually with fine cymbidium clones as well as the export of flowers.

Part of the impetus from the beginning was the air freighting of cymbidium flowers from Australia to other parts of the world. Initially small, the trade grew and became a large overseas earning source. This led the hybridist to produce a spike and flower specifically to satisfy the demand. One such is illustrated in the pictorial section.

The period between 1950 and 1970 was intensely interesting so far as development of cymbidium hybridising in Australia was concerned, because those years bracketed the development of virtually a completely new strain, not all from Australian parents but with many included.

# Planning the pastime of orchid growing

Several areas of populated Australia are unsuitable for growing cymbidiums and those garden lovers looking toward them as a pastime or hobby should be careful of the types they buy.

In the miniature group several of the breeding species should produce plants which would adapt, including both *Cymbidium sauve* and *Cymbidium canaliculatum*. While there are few hybrids from these or *Cymbidium madidum,* there is no reason why hybridists should not concentrate on them to supply miniature cymbidiums which would fit better into lowland semi-tropical areas.

Unlike the east coast area of Australia from Eden, on about latitude 38 degrees south to about latitude 28 degrees, the ideal area for cymbidium cultivation, where the climate is of wet summer season and dry winter, the southern parts of Australia have a reverse climate of dry summers and wet winters.

That oversimplification may cause a smile on some faces, but we must generalise a little. The east coast suits cymbidiums while that of the south must have some control to get the same results. Any other areas with similar patterns should also note this. It all hinges on the associated factor of humidity. Where the east coast has it at the right time to suit the genus, the south has it when the plants least need it or when they should be a little dryer.

None of these things are barriers which cannot be overcome, but the frequency of flowering and the period which spikes take to mature and open varies a lot from place to place and from grower to grower. In frost-free areas minimum shelter is adequate, but in an area where frosts are frequent cymbidiums will come almost to a halt in growth as well as flowering stages. This non-continuity of flower development always goes against quality as well as size and shape.

Some cymbidium cultivators and even botanists contend that cymbidium hybrids are a product of their environment and need continuity of the conditions under which they began life. While that may be an overstatement of fact, there is an element of truth in it. It is unreal to imagine continuing the sort of existence in a flask which a seedling has as it germinates and grows, but humidity and shelter as a part of that process must continue. Some planning along those lines is natural, even if the plants to be grown are few and under shade trees. If there are climatic restrictions above or below the flexible limits they should also be allowed for.

The ideal temperature limits for growing cymbidiums are between 18 to 27 degrees Celsius (65 to 80 degrees Fahrenheit), while for flowering the ideal temperature range lies between 13 to 22 degrees Celsius (55 to 70 degrees Fahrenheit). Celsius is a rather coarse scale to use for orchid growing because a mere two or three degrees Fahrenheit could mean the difference between growing an orchid or losing it. These two temperature ranges could well apply as summer and winter cultural ideals as those are the seasons for growth and flowering. Most cymbidiums would drop their buds if flowering temperatures go too high. Neither range can be expected to be constant, as fairly wide variations occur from time to time in short bursts.

How to counteract adverse conditions and undue rises in temperature depends on whether the plants are grown in open air or under glass-house conditions.

In a glass-house the answer lies in shade, ventilation and humidity and this is one reason for advising a minimum size to aim for in construction. Ease of control has a great deal of influence on growing and flowering cymbidiums.

12

Outdoor-grown plants may be cooled by using a lot more water than in a glass-house because it will cause its own air circulation to aid cooling. Cymbidiums grown outdoors could have a constant fine spray drifting over them on hot days provided they have sun protection, but the foliage will quickly burn if left open to excess light. It was not until heavy watering was adopted in some of the hotter parts of Australia that cymbidiums appeared to have much chance. To some degree it is almost impossible to overwater them in summer in those conditions.

At the cold end of the scale the variations should be much less. While an occasional lapse into the 4 to 5 degrees Celsius range (35 to 40 degrees Fahrenheit) does not do much harm if the plants are dry, they should not be expected to flower if this lapse is a feature of their winter culture.

In the instance of frost-prone areas, part of the planning should be for some type of heating for glass-house growing unless the glass-house is fairly large — in the 15 metres by 5 metres range — or of giving up growing cymbidiums altogether, as they are frost-prone in severe conditions. The leaves quickly develop black patches. If only a few plants are grown in frost-prone areas and they are grown outdoors they may be taken into a shed or some form of shelter during the winter nights and put outdoors again first thing in the morning. So much extra work would perhaps take some of the fun out of the pastime, but at least it may save the flower spikes.

There can be no more frustrating waste of time than growing cymbidium plants year after year without flowering them. It is very easy to convert a growing cymbidium into a flowering plant in ideal conditions, but there is no doubt that those growers bypassed by success did not realise in the first place what the plants needed. Sometimes, too, they were possibly misled by people who really knew little about the plants they sold.

If automation is within reach financially it is very useful, particularly for cooling when necessary and warming when that is needed. It may seem too technical an approach, but if all the functions are properly installed they cut out human error or miscalculation and take care of things when no one is about. Instead of going off to work and telling the lady of the house what to do, the man of the house, instead of frothing about what may have been impossible for the lady, just sets the switches and controls and goes off to work and forgets about it all. Except for a power failure there is no problem. If it is the lady who gives the orders then the man-about-the-house also has no worries. A lot of advice about these facilities is available from most of the electricity authorities, who have special departments to deal with such inquiries.

When starting to grow cymbidiums it is not always necessary to know where they came from or anything much about them except how to grow them. But as it is part of their background it often helps to know why they grow as they do and how differently they must be treated from garden plants to fit them into our scheme of things. There are many societies throughout various countries which specialise in orchids and they all contain potential friends with whom to talk things over.

As plants cymbidiums are really epiphytes — plants which commonly grow on trees and rock surfaces, but are not parasites like other things such as mistletoe, the roots of which penetrate into and rob their host tree.

Some cymbidiums also grow as terrestrial or saprophytic plants on the surface of the land, living always on decaying vegetation. True terrestrial orchids seldom grow in earth or 'dirt' as we know it.

As with the Australian cymbidiums, the best plants are found growing in hollow ends of limbs and in knot-holes in trees, the roots penetrating the hollow and decaying interior of the trees, frequently filling the cavity, the leaves forming a draining system into the interior to further introduce rainwater to reduce the heartwood to plant food. Forks of trees are also convenient perches for cymbidiums, the plant forming a food trap to hold decaying vegetation. This, of course, is a totally different form of cymbidium growth to our unnatural methods, but it gives a lead to the material cymbidiums live on.

But think for a moment of the chance germination of a cymbidium seed, which is so small as to be almost invisible to the naked eye, when it falls into the right place to germinate in a forest environment. That so small a thing could grow into such a large plant is almost unbelievable. In its turn this large plant falls into the forest floor and itself decays and feeds the growing things in a cycle that has been going on for perhaps millions of years.

Cymbidiums are grown almost as terrestrial plants in our artificial mediums, but the basic ingredient should still be decaying vegetable matter. This is the only aspect in which our cultivation runs parallel to natural processes. We can induce them with such things as artificial fertilisers into the flowering stage, but only if certain things are first satisfied.

There is a balance between root and leaf area in healthy pot-grown cymbidiums. In experimental measurements which I made some years ago of a cymbidium plant of six green bulbs, two back-bulbs and one leading growth, the roots were all cut off and measured and then the leaves were measured. There was 25 metres (82 feet) of root in sections of from 61 centimetres (24 inches) down to offshoots of 2.54 centimetres (1 inch). Of that 25 metres, 17.7 metres (58 feet) was of good working root, the remaining 7.3 metres (24 feet) dead or non-viable root. The total leaf length from the point of dehiscence, where they are cast or break off, was 25.3 metres (83 feet), or about the same length as the viable root and the non-viable root. The comparative working surface area of both roots and leaves was in almost perfect balance.

The experiment was carried out on other plants and in all instances where the plant was healthy and growing well the balance was always there. It was rather expensive on plants but at least it proved something to me.

One of the problems found in some of the complex hybrids is an imbalance along these lines, so that leaf vigor is not matched by root vigor and careful cultivation is needed with them. They also seem prone to exhibit signs of this imbalance in leaf markings and blotches not unlike those usually seen in virus-infected plants. They seem to be problem plants right from the seedling stage.

The conditions under which they are to be grown should dictate selection of clones. If they are to be grown as garden plants, or even as cymbidiums expected to endure extreme variations in weather, it would be unwise to select high-priced clones or exhibition-type flowers. Above all, if you intend to start growing cymbidiums this way, do not start off with back-bulbs. They may be less expensive, but they have so limited a potential as hard-grown plants and it may be so long a time until they flower that the grower becomes disillusioned, even in good climates. Exceptions have been known, but they are infrequent.

As in all human activities some successful individuals expect everyone to be as clever as they are. Basically this is applicable to growing cymbidiums and although they are at times successfully grown in ways that break all the rules, not everyone can do that. It is the exception that proves the rule. Perhaps we have all heard that one, too.

Natural conditions are always best for growing cymbidiums and the word 'environment' describes them. They only grow naturally in a good environment. It is a word which has been used more in the last twenty or so years than at any other period. For cymbidium growers the word is significant across a whole range of places in Australia and other countries. If not considered at all the project is rather pointless. Environment is a combination of many things, starting with climate, natural or artificial, then light, protection from influences which may affect growth or flowering, and including watering and association with other plants to give 'atmosphere'.

In total outdoor culture, including flowering, the results will be poor occasionally compared with what can be obtained with sheltered arrangements. While some places have a good natural environment, others lack it completely. Perhaps the best way to begin would be to outline something for the grower who has a few plants and lives in a climate which is borderline rather than ideally suiting cymbidiums.

The ideal is one which is warm and humid in the growing period but cools off in the flowering season, such as that of coastal New South Wales. A grower living in a moderate climate, however much it may suit other plants, with a dry summer and a cold and wet winter, has problems; particularly if that climate has long periods of hot weather in the cymbidium growing season. Elevation moderates tropical and semi-tropical areas so that at 750 to 1000 metres above sea level climates can be found which suit cymbidiums. It is not wise to be dogmatic about any latitude or any area, but rather to be encouraging, so that everyone who would like to try them could at least have a go.

In all these climates shade is a first consideration. The period during the day in which the plants get speckled sunlight is the first thing to look at, and associated with this the direction in which they face. It is called 'aspect'. One of the best aspects for cymbidiums is direct sunlight in the first hours of the day, speckled sunlight for the following few hours, with the hottest period offering shade. This is ideal for growth and flowering. Night climate comes into it too, because plants exposed to frost become retarded and the leaves and flowers blemish. Cymbidiums are, after all, originally used to a soft climate, even if cold at night.

One plant is not enough on which to base a cultural program and as soon as possible a small collection of flowering and unflowering plants should be built up so that differences and similarities can be seen and understood. Growing one cymbidium is like growing one petunia in a flower bed and expecting a show and also learning how to grow them.

If a good aspect cannot be found for cymbidiums the project should be ended, because cymbidiums need light, most particularly when growing. In outdoor culture speckled sunlight for spring, summer and autumn is needed. Trees, if used to give this speckled sunlight, should be chosen carefully. Some, such as pines, willows, some eucalypts and any other densely leafed trees should be avoided. Deciduous trees are not always suitable either, because the leaf pattern changes too abruptly and permanent foliage is at least some protection from frost.

The aspect of some places is sterile and unfriendly. A veranda, for instance, without the influence of other plants in pots; a sunroom with a cymbidium standing on its own in a corner; or a single plant standing against a wall or out on a path or any other similar situation which may be thought up. Always try to give cymbidiums a 'plant-growing environment'. However much you may have heard or read about how easy they are to grow, I always say the opposite — they are hard to grow but look easy. I also believe in encouraging people to learn how to grow them. There are probably thousands of dissatisfied cymbidium growers, frustrated more by the lack of flowers than for any other reason. Some of this is induced by lack of environment, which must always be created. It seldom exists unaided.

Starting at the growing season, which is from October to March, the plants should be correctly potted in a good growing medium. If they need dividing and starting off again it should be done in this period, preferably at the beginning to the middle of it. The type of pot used is immaterial, but if plastic pots are used all the plants should be in plastic pots. Do not mix them in clay and plastic pots. If they are of different sizes the smallest will dry out first. Put them where they can be seen.

During the growing season, and even at times throughout the year, cymbidiums will send up shoots from the sides of the older bulbs. These are called new leads and in time will develop into fully matured bulbs. Sometimes it may take up to two seasons to develop this far and into flowering in outdoor culture, particularly in latitudes 36 to 39 degrees south, which can be found on any school atlas. Below these latitudes outdoor growing becomes a rather chancy thing.

As these bulbs grow they may produce either new growths or flower spikes from the base of the immature bulbs within or without the short outer sheathing leaves at the sides. Mostly they burst through the sides as they emerge. The difference between growth and flower spikes is shown in the illustrations. Experience soon gives confidence to predictions for growth or flower.

It is sometimes difficult to tell which is which, but the best way is to be patient until they are taller and then there is no mistaking them. The new growths part in the centre to expose growing leaves and the spikes elongate into thick pencil-like spikes which will have soft tips. Do not squeeze these tips too hard when feeling them. Spikes mostly show up between February and April. Frequently when these new growths are sufficiently exposed it is plain which are growth and flower spikes, as the growths are nearly always somewhat flattened and triangular lengthwise, while the spikes are rounded and always look like the blunt tip of a pencil even when immature.

If flower spikes are there, resist the temptation to take plants into the house. They are best left outside where they will get sunlight and some shelter from frost. When finally they are taken inside they should be grown in a sunroom or a light window where they can get sunlight. They should be put outside for most of the day, particularly when it rains. This form of cultivation means a lot of work, but usually the flowers are worth it.

If the collection of plants is larger, say up to twenty or more, and the growing system is open-air, a small shelter of plastic sheeting over wire-netting or shade-cloth is a good way of sheltering the plants from rain and cold and all the other things which may affect maturing and flowering of the spikes.

Usually outdoor flowering means later flowers than from plants grown in permanent shelter like a glass-house. If early-flowering hybrids are selected then what should be early will be mid-season flowering and they will appear in August and September.

The majority of cymbidium growers seem to start off with a piece of a plant given to them by a friend and do not understand what it needs. All too frequently this piece is a back-bulb and is unsuitable as a starter. It may not even have growth eyes at the base as it should. The receiver of this doubtful gift should get hold of something more substantial if results are wanted.

Climate and aspect are no less important for the next group, which starts off with something a little better than completely outdoor growing and back-bulbs, even if most rudimentary. It is surprising how many of this next group are beneficiaries under wills of deceased orchid growers. (I sometimes wonder what will become of mine.)

The cheapest form of shelter is little less expensive than the dearest. Both start off

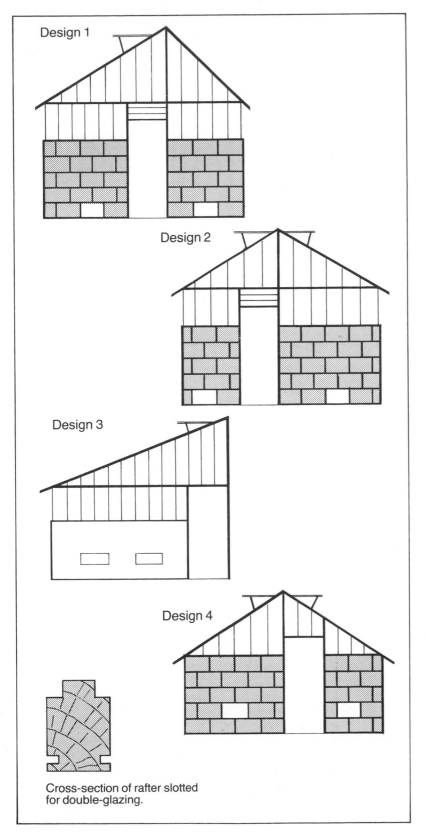

Design 1

Design 2

Design 3

Design 4

Cross-section of rafter slotted
for double-glazing.

# Glass-house Designs

**Design 1:** For situations where an east-west glass-house is necessary. The longer slope of the roof to the north gives better light to the back of the glass-house. This type is suitable for epiphytes or cymbidiums, the glazed sides admitting plenty of light to the benches. The ventilators are shown at ground level but may be varied. The louvre above the door may be left open or closed, but the top ventilator, shown in the open position, should be open to some degree at all times.

**Design 2:** This is the ideal type for epiphytes or cymbidiums where the glass-house runs north and south. Roof ventilators are fitted to both sides of this structure and the lower ventilators may be put into the second course of bricks if desired. If fans are fitted inside either of the No. 1 or No. 2 designs they should be inside the louvres above the door and if the air flow is too rapid the top ventilators may be closed down to baffle it. The bottom ventilators should be fitted with slides to close them if necessary and fly-wire to keep out the pests.

**Design 3:** This is the lean-to type designed to fit against an existing wall or on to a constructed wall facing the north. Side-wall windows may be fitted or not, depending on the type of orchids grown. This type of glass-house is adaptable to any genera and would be particularly effective for odontoglossums, paphio-pedilums, cattleyas or phalaenopsis, to mention a few. Its advantages stem mainly from its orientation facing the north. The design is easy to build, shade and heat, particularly if double glazing is used. Ventilator and louvre positions are optional. A cavity wall of fibro-cement sheeting suits this design.

**Design 4:** This type of glass-house has the advantage of eliminating glazing in side walls. It also is suitable to certain types of orchids but not others. It should preferably be facing east and west so that the sun penetrates both sides at morning or afternoon. It is an ideal type for paphiopedilums and other shade-loving orchids. Again ventilator and louvre positions are optional, but roof ventilators should be on both sides.

17

with some type of frame holding up a covering and sheltering medium such as the various shade-cloths, plastic or glass. There are many different ways of putting them up, even of converting outdoor sheds to glass-houses. Some ideas may germinate from studying the illustrations.

The aspect, if in a garden, should be where most sunlit hours are possible, particularly morning sunlight. If sunlight is severely restricted it would be better to convert to some other type of orchids which do not need so much direct sunlight.

As cymbidiums are large plants and do best when spread out so that the leaves can develop fully, whatever is planted should take up as much space as possible.

Starting with some simple form of shelter, shade-cloth erected on a frame for instance, it should be at least two and a half metres above the ground. It may be flat-roofed like the one illustrated, or it can be of gable-roofed or lean-to design. Shade-cloth lasts a lot longer if put up over wire-netting. Despite the original cost, the whole construction will be stronger. Shade-cloth may be tied to wire-netting with plastic-coated wire 'twisties'.

There is no restriction on the area which may be covered in this fashion and some of the largest of such structures cover acres of ground, not all, however, given over to cymbidium cultivation. If not filled with cymbidiums, the climate of these shaded areas is improved by the number and variety of plants grown, such as ferns, shrubs, palms and house-plant types. They add to the humidity necessary with increased sunlight and warmer temperatures.

Ground cover of wood chips, bark, screenings, coke-ash or any water-retaining aggregate is frequently used to add to the humidity. To retain this ground cover and keep out some of the pests, a low retaining plinth around the area is a good idea as it will give an anchorage for the walls if they are of shade-cloth. The plinth may be of fibro-cement sheet, wood or any other material. This is an advantage in windy areas, where so much damage can be caused to buds by wind-blown foliage. It is surprising how even shade-cloth breaks its force.

Naturally, this type of growing shelter or the primary outdoor type of tree shelter is more suitable to places where the mean temperature does not fall to frost level in winter but is also temperate in summer. In hot, dry climates some modifications should be included to maintain humidity. These could be automatic, such as overhead sprinklers with a time control, or even manually operated. The relatively low cost is well worth it where plants are left to themselves for most of the day. Shade would also need to be thorough. Very few places have weather patterns which may be relied on throughout the year and innovations should be thought up to suit individually designed shelter areas in different localities.

Sometimes attempts are made to grow cymbidiums where they should not be expected to grow, but if the right provision is made, sometimes expensive, the difficulties may be overcome. Cymbidiums are essentially temperate zone plants and the project would seem futile, even if only to prove a point. There is no way of heating or warming semi-open enclosures to allow cymbidium culture in frost-prone climates. Perhaps the plants may survive and start off again in the warmer months, but again the project is inadvisable, as when the plants are ready to flower the conditions will cancel out this part of their cycle.

Outdoor culture and primitive shelter have one thing in common — there is little need to worry about benches for the plants. There must be some sorting out, however, so that the larger plants do not overshadow the smaller ones and retard them.

Lastly, for those growers who choose this outdoor type of growing, there is no way any set of guidelines can be laid down about how to grow cymbidiums. If the plants do not react favorably in the conditions applied and produce some flowers, then it is toward the next group that growers should look and become owners of some form of totally enclosed and climate-controlled area.

Putting up a totally enclosed area where there is scope for climate control needs more planning for aspect than any of the more primitive systems. In the first place, a local building authority's permit is necessary.

The spot chosen should be sunlit for most of the day, with emphasis on morning sunlight. The plan should be for a north-south alignment. It may be any one of the illustrated designs, but in all instances the distance from the roof to the plant should be not less than 1.5 to 2 metres. It is unreal to lay down a minimum glass-house size for cymbidiums, as they will grow in most glass-houses. Overcrowding, however, goes against flowering and the larger a glass-house can be designed and built the better. If it came to a dogmatic statement of minimum size, it could be about 3.5 metres by 2.5 metres and not less than 2.5 metres high. It is much harder to maintain temperature or humidity levels at an even figure in a small glass-house, however much time is put into it.

Glass-houses operate in a special way. The warmth from the sun enters the roof and walls in the form of radiation even on cloudy days. The warmth is trapped inside by the glass, which is a poor conductor of heat. The plants use sunlight to carry out their functions of growing and flowering quite independently of the warmth it provides to keep them moving. The climate inside is affected by the type of plants, their density and the moisture they absorb. A completely new environment, different to that outside, must be created. This is the main difference between this system and that of outdoor and primitive cultivation.

There is a great amount of variation in design, materials and inside layout. The walls may be of brick, preferably absorbent types such as cinder bricks, or fibro-cement sheet on a wooden frame or any other sheathing which will protect the plants and allow environmental planning inside. Brick walls would remain warm longer than single fibro-cement sheet walls. But if this material is used for an inside and outside sheathing, the air pocket between the two would be a good heat trap, improved if the space between the two sheaths is filled with sawdust or some other form of insulating packing. If the gap is filled, the filling should be kept dry to avoid rotting.

Ventilation should be a consideration. Some designers prefer ventilation in the upper part of the walls, others like to have it low, but some ventilation should also be provided in the roof.

Provided there is a good flow of air in the warmer period of the year and scope for shutting it off a little in cold weather, any system is suitable.

An electric fan system can be built in to provide air movement. While some orchids will thrive with circulation of the air enclosed in the glass-house with a small amount of fresh air admitted, cymbidiums seem to prefer a very fast replacement of the air from outside in the growing season and during bud formation and opening. If this air can be humidified so much the better.

If for some reason, such as fencing or other baffling factors, a good circulation is prevented, a fan should be installed low down in the glass-house and large diameter plastic tubing ducts fixed to take the air flow. At intervals along the ducting, holes should be cut out so that the air can be vented at various points. The end of the duct should be tied off so that a partial air compression is caused to keep the duct inflated. Duct diameter should be not less than about 30 centimetres. If it is fitted above the plants the holes should be cut in the underside to give a down-draught. The plastic ducting is obtainable from plastic sheet processors and any small type of fan will keep it inflated. It should be correctly wired in accordance with the standards of local electricity authorities. That should also be the case for any of the electrics installed in a glass-house.

Benching the plants should be dictated by the height of the walls. If there is plenty of light coming in at plant level when they are benched near the floor then a great deal of labor and material can be saved. If the walls are solid up to the roof, benches would be better staged about halfway. Thus, if the walls are 1.5 metres high (about 5 feet) then the benches should be about 50 centimetres above the floor.

There are two types of benches, solid or slatted. The solid type is suitable for some orchids which do not need so much air flow and the slatted type more suitable for cymbidiums because of the increased upward air flow they allow about the plants, particularly if ventilators are installed low down in the walls.

Weldmesh or concrete reinforcing mesh makes excellent benching, either galvanised or black. The black is less expensive and lasts very well. It needs some timber or pipe framing to hold it as it is too flexible to be used without support. The mesh should be about 50 millimetres by 80 millimetres, made up of 5 millimetres gauge wire.

Easy access to every plant should be allowed for, planning the entry and paths so that there are no deep corners where plants cannot be examined and watered easily.

All of these recommendations are ideals to be aimed at, but various innovations can be worked in as individiual ideas, particularly in relation to the building itself.

When planning heating or warming systems for glass-houses in climates where it is needed there are several types to choose from. Some, such as kerosene or electric heaters, apply heat direct to the interior. Other electric heaters act through radiation units in tubes. Gas, oil, or electric furnaces are made to heat circulating water in pipes about the glass-house.

Unless a system is based on one already installed and working well, it is best to consult manufacturers or their agents for information. It is rare to find an installation fulfilling its role to complete satisfaction at first, so always be prepared to modify it by making benches and other fittings easily dismantled.

If kerosene is used in a heater it should have a flue to take out some or all of the heating gases generated. Frequently these contain unburnt residues which can distort and destroy flower buds. These heaters are the easiest to install and use, but they are possibly the worst selection because they are not automatic and require constant cleaning and wick trimming, even the blue-flame type. Nevertheless, a special greenhouse heater is made for this purpose and I have seen them used with no ill effects at all. In this instance, however, their maintenance was faultless.

First expenses are usually high when oil or gas-fired boilers are installed. Fuel expenses for either would balance out about the same and either type is readily obtainable.

Electricity is probably the most expensive, but it can be automated a little easier than other systems. Thermostatic controls can be fitted to all the systems, but there is nothing mechanical about the electrical system and it simply switches on or off at previously set limits. It may also be used to control ventilation, humidity and watering, which may suit some of the very busy people.

It is not possible to give reliable estimates about running costs for any of the heating systems, but one thing is certain — the sellers of these units qualify for the title of supreme optimists and the first bills usually shock the budget-conscious housewife if not the orchid grower. The blow is softened by the appearance of nice clean, well-shaped flowers and in cold climates this is the surest way to get them.

There are several things which may soften the shock of heating expenses. One is using wooden glazing bars instead of metal, with a slot cut out 50 millimetres below the rebate in which the glass roof is puttied. Sheets of the same glass as the roof are slid up this slot, creating an air gap which is a very effective insulator. In order to slide the sheets up the rafter to the ridge the slot at one side of the wall end of the rafter is cut away and a sealing strip nailed up as the last sheet is put into place. This may cut the heating bill by about one-third.

Inside liners of polythene film beneath the glass, plastic or fibreglass roof is a second-best way to do the same thing, but it will not cut the bills as much. In most glass-houses a little ingenuity with wires and hooks gives an anchorage and this inside liner should last two or three seasons. Many of the modern glass-houses are kit-form types designed to take single layers of glass with little scope for double lining. Even these can be modified in some way.

Never be tempted to close down the ventilation in the belief that this will trap the warmth already in the glass-house. It does not hold it for long and this practice will cause more problems than it solves.

For the handy man or woman — after all, we are men and women, not persons — the kit-form glass-houses are quite easy to handle and erect. They should preferably be erected on a base, concrete or redgum, and all instructions come with them. They are freely advertised in most garden magazines and some appear in telephone directories.

Some timbers if used in glass-houses quickly rot in the humidity and types should be selected which withstand it, such as redgum or treated pine. Durability of these is increased if thoroughly painted with old sump oil, particularly if they contact the earth or the walls if they are built of bricks. Do not use untreated wood or unsuitable wood for benching, as it will soon decay, even if soaked with sump oil. If treated timber is used, allowance should be made for it as an innovation for which much is claimed. However, it may be used for cavity walls using fibro-cement sheeting, for wall plates on top of brick walls, or for double-glazed roofing members.

If glass is used on the roof the overlap should be kept to a maximum of about 5 millimetres. Too large an overlap fills with dirt and other harmful things like fungus spores, tends to cut down light intensity in cloudy weather, and creates a condensation trap which may cause drips on the plants and set up brown rot infections.

How far into glass-house provision an individual goes should depend first on the prevailing climate, the results expected from the plants, and the area available. Once a glass-house is put up, however, it is reasonably easy to adapt it to orchids other than cymbidiums if they are found unsuitable or become tiresome.

# Growing Enclosures

Orchid growing can commence indoors with smaller plants like Slippers but is scarcely possible with such large things as cymbidiums. This growing case is totally controlled by electricity. The Grolux fluorescent lamps come on at certain times and are switched off after a lapse of anything up to about sixteen hours. The case is warmed by electric elements and the fan is also under control for either recirculating the air contained in the cabinet or admitting a certain amount of room air. An installation like this should be stood in a room which has good ventilation so that it is not just the stagnant house air which is fanned through the plants. Watering is manual, but may be indicated with 'prods' to test the moisture in the potting mix or by a hygrometer or humidity gauge placed in the cabinet.

The glass-house is almost indispensable for orchid growing in most climates. This is a simply constructed type, about 2.5 metres high. The bricks are cement and cinder, very porous and perhaps a little fragile in ground inclined to shift, but quite effective with a good foundation. The glazing is simplified by using galvanised glazing bars in both walls and roof. Bottom ventilation is not included in this house because of the gap left where the glazing bars are fixed to the walls, which gives a permanent air flow. But the roof ventilation consists of a top section on the ridge which may be raised and lowered. A glass-house like this, if heated by any of the conventional or unconventional means such as a fan heater (electric) or a kerosene heater designed for green-houses, would be suitable for most genera. 5.5 by 4 metres, it suits a moderate sized backyard. A council permit should be sought before erecting any glass-house.

Ventilation is one of the most important things to arrange in construction, both in the roof and the walls. Louvres such as illustrated are better than opening sash windows because even when they are shut there is a certain amount of entry between the glass louvres. The upper ventilation should be such that a good flow is possible for the whole length of a glass-house such as this. While this glass-house is painted, other forms of shading are possible and in the centre foreground Sarlon shade-cloth has been added to the paint and held in place at the bottom with clothes pegs.

Overall shading with woven plastic cloths of various values is sufficient for some genera, but in the instances where it may not be, the glass should be painted in addition. It is possible to buy various grades of shade-cloth to block out as much as 70 to 80 per cent of direct light and they should be selected to suit both the orchids cultivated and the relative climates and positions of a glass-house. While it may also be used as an interior lining, it is better to stretch it over an external frame such as this.

Any type of orchid may be grown in an outdoor shelter such as this, naturally depending on location. In warm climates the selection is not so restricted as in cooler climates. The construction is simple. It is built from two full sheets of concrete reinforcing mesh set on to a heavy wooden plinth, the ends being fabricated from another sheet. The finished igloo-like structure is covered with shade-cloth of fairly heavy texture. Perhaps the greatest struggle will be in persuading the flat sheets of mesh to bend into shape, but this is easily done by pulling them into form with a couple of pieces of rope. This type of structure allows for considerable innovation and perhaps some of the smarter people may be able to think up easy ways to do it all. It is also made easier if a small electric welder is available.

This type of growing shade house is fairly easy for handy people to put up. It is fabricated from 1.25 cm (½ inch) galvanised piping and the clips made for clamping sections together. The tea-tree stake side gives good ventilation, but any of the sides exposed to rough weather may be covered in with fibre-glass or plastic corrugated sheeting or the whole structure may be covered with wire-netting and then shade-cloth or the shade-cloth tied straight on to the piping with 'twisties'. A simple wooden plinth around the bottom gives a fixing for the wall materials and if required wooden battens may be attached to the pipe with saddle-clips.

Where space is no object a roofed enclosure like this is an ideal cymbidium shelter in most climates. It is erected in 1.90 cm (¾ inch) piping clipped together and covered in shade-cloth. The height of the structure over the plants gives some idea of the clearance needed between the roof and the plants on the ground. The shade-cloth would need careful selection in building a structure this size, as a mistake could be costly. In very sunny climates it could go as high as 80 per cent shade. There is no limit to the size of these pipe structures and they are ideal where outdoor cymbidium cultivation is possible.

For many exotic species and hybrids in cooler centres some form of artificial heating is necessary in winter. Originally coke- or coal-fired boilers were used to heat water circulating in pipes throughout glass-houses. They were large and cumbersome and the fuel had an ash residue which had to be disposed of. In later years oil-fired boilers were produced which were both smaller and easier to control. This Pottington oil- or gas-fired boiler is one such. No fuel, whether gas, oil or electrical energy is cheap to run and this is where double glazing with either glass or plastic sheeting helps out. With artificial and automated heating some form of humidifying equipment is almost essential.

The control box of an automatic humidifier. The flat gauze leaf protruding from the back of the box is the receptor for the fogger nozzles set into the water pipe running the length of the glass-house. One of the nozzles may be seen alongside the edge of the white tray containing the plants. When operating, the whole lower area of the glass-house is shrouded with a fine misting spray. This fog settles on the flat gauze activator and when it is loaded with water it sinks and turns off the control switch. As soon as it dries it rises again on a counter-balance and the fogging cycle commences all over again.

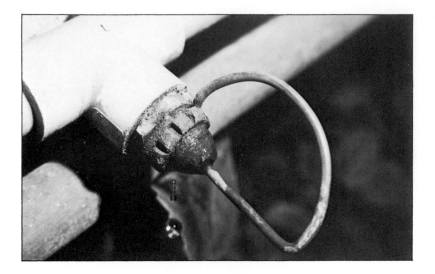

A close-up of one of the fogger nozzles, with a drop of water falling away from it. In operation a fine jet of water impinges on the surface of the end of the bent wire and breaks up into a fine fog. There are many types of foggers, but they all work on this principle, some of them with a temperature overrider so that even if the humidity drops when the temperature is low they will not operate. In addition to automatic heat control, these humidifiers cancel out a lot of manual cultivation control and allow latitude for busy people.

Air circulation in confined growing spaces is vital for the health of the plants. The position of fans for circulating air is best decided by the type of benches used and the amount of ventilation given the plants. With Slippers a large amount of fresh air is not necessary, but there should always be a certain amount of 'new' air admitted day and night. In order that all the plants get their share a fan is used to distribute it. If a closed bench system is built in, a fan should be set fairly high in the glass-house like the illustration, but if an open bench system is used the fan should be low in the glass-house so that the air can be given an upward flow under the benches and through the plants.

In glass-houses where only moderate or occasional heating is necessary this illustrated type is one of the simplest. It is a galvanised or sheet metal box 1 metre high and 75 cm square in which an ordinary blue-flame kerosene heater is installed. The 15-centimetre duct is made of galvanised sheet metal and runs the length of the glass-house, exhausting at the far end, by this means avoiding the toxic effects of the combustion fumes. Although the warmth is rather localised along the length of the duct, which has a slight upward slope from the box, it is sufficiently effective to break the effects of a frosty night. Several variations may also be thought up. Although rather primitive, it is better than nothing at all. An aperture at the bottom of the box is necessary to admit air for the heater, preferably fitted with a control slide to adjust the flow-through. It should also be lined with insulation to prevent an external hot-spot.

# Protection and Shading

While it may seem a remote possibility at the time, damage to the roof from hail or any other cause should be considered and a spare sheet of plastic or fibreglass carried if that is used, or twenty to thirty sheets of the same glass as covers the roof put away in a box in case of accidents. In some areas hailstorms are common and to avoid damage 10 millimetre wire-netting should be used as a roof cover. It should be framed about 30 centimetres above the roof. With some prefabricated glass-houses this framing is supplied as an option and it makes fixing shade-cloth or blinds much simpler.

Glass-house shading is more trouble than adjusting plants to take outdoor conditions because the foliage never grows quite as hard and light resistant. Inadequate shade is usually indicated by lightening of the foliage and perhaps burning on areas of the leaves where they bend over, facing directly to the roof. It also causes fast dehydration of the glass-house. Too dense shading has the opposite effect of producing lush deep green foliage and humidity over and above that required. While too much light may not affect flowering, too little most probably will.

There are three general systems of shading: painting with water paint, shade-cloth or hessian scrim, or roller blinds made of wooden slats. They are somewhat in this order of expense too.

Water paint should be used, not oil. Several brands are available and if they are thinned or mixed with milk and water the paint stays on much longer. It does not matter whether the milk is powder or liquid natural milk. The paint should be thoroughly mixed and can be put on with a broom, paint brush, stirrup pump or any other way which gives a good even coat. Choose a sunny day and do it in the morning so that by nightfall the paint has hardened. Always use white paint, not creamy colored.

Shade-cloth should be bought in a density to suit the area, which may need anything up to about 80 per cent or as little as 50 per cent shade. It may be best to start at about 60 per cent shade and change up or down as the results indicate on the foliage. Pale, yellow-green leaves show that the percentage is too light, while dark green foliage would indicate that it is too heavy. Do not leave any gaps where the sun may get through and burn the leaves, particularly if they are wet.

Sometimes a combination of painting and shade-cloth suits the situation. The side walls, if glazed, should be painted.

Lath blinds give the best shade of all, either horizontally or vertically rolled depending on the type of glass-house. The traversing sun gives a good pattern on the leaves, but the gap between the laths is critical. It should not exceed 5 millimetres with 15 millimetre wide laths. These lath blinds are more suited to moderate climates than to hotter, more exposed, climates. Unlike shade-cloth, they are permanent; the first expense is the last except for an occasional oiling or painting to preserve the wood. They also need piping or timber framing, but should be constructed so that they will roll over wire-netting.

Hessian scrim blinds are the easiest to put up because the material may be tied directly on the roof with no gap between the plastic sheeting or glass. These blinds, however, must be removed in long periods of cloudy weather or in the autumn. No direct sunlight gaps should be left.

All of these shade mediums can be combined if it suits, and it will be found that they will need to be varied with the type of material used on the roof. Some of the plastic corrugated sheeting is tinted, but this tinting is impermanent and may not be adequate on some days. It is impossible to recommend any tint because what suits one area will not suit another. However, yellow or pale pink should be avoided, and a selection made of the blues and greens, preferably light tints. Dense colors of any kind will inhibit growth and flowering and may not suit some of the flower colors.

Some growers may find it suits their construction better to have the shade attached inside the roof rather than on the outside and there is also no general rule to cover this. It is unusual to strike the right combination initially and it may take a few seasons to stabilise to a system which suits.

Whatever shade is used should be progressively reduced from about the beginning of March in moderate climates, later for the hotter areas. This is where the advantage of the painted glass roof shows up. The paint should first be scratched over with a coarse broom at the beginning of March, letting a little more direct sunlight on to the plants. Even the grower under the trees gets this automatically as the leaf starts to thin out over his plants. Toward the end of March the broom should be run over the roof again and at the beginning of April the glass should be almost half clear, the paint almost entirely gone by the end of April. If the paint is hard to shift it can be softened with a spray over with a hose or broomed down on a rainy day. Either way is slightly messy, but it should all be cleaned off before another coat is put on the following summer. Growers with tinted plastic roofing using shade-cloth should have it all off by the end of April too. Those using only shade-cloth over untinted glass, plastic or fibreglass should at least change over to a very light cloth.

Correct light plays a big part in getting the right color into the flowers. Some growers recommend leaving the plants where the spikes were formed until they are hardened, others sort them out into groups of different colors for variety of shading, with the unflowering plants closed up to make room for those flowering.

Green-flowered cymbidiums certainly need more shade than reds and pinks from the time the buds show at the tip of the spikes. They should be given light shade so they do not develop a dark streak down the backs of the upper sepals.

Cymbidium buds are resupinate, like most orchids. They develop immaturely on the spike with the lower part of the flower, enclosing the labellum, toward the main stem, turning through an angle of 180 degrees as they mature so that the dorsal sepal is uppermost and the labellum below as the flowers open. Shading for green cymbidiums through the whole of this process ensures that the color is green and not bronze, even on the outer surfaces of the flower.

At the time the buds are opening the shade should be so dense that the flowers do not get direct light at all. But do not imagine they will open in the dark, although, strangely enough, that is the period when well grown and cultured flowers go through most of this process.

Pink and red cymbidiums will tolerate quite bright light until the buds begin to open, when they also should be well shaded and, like the greens, cooled as they open. Some growers like direct sun for their reds and pinks, but most prefer speckled sunlight.

Yellow and white cymbidium flowers have to be light-processed to suit the area where they are grown, as there is a great amount of variation in light intensity from the sun in different states.

There is always a certain amount of disappointment in flowering cymbidiums when they do not measure up to the specimens which prompted purchase of the clones. It is a natural thing, because frequently certain cymbidiums do far better in one climate than another and also frequently the purchaser does not build up a plant vigorous enough to equal that on which he saw the flowers.

Each hybrid cymbidium has its own individual bulb shape and size, the limits of which are usually reached in a 25 centimetres pot. Some may never produce large bulbs, others go beyond the average. Size signifies little, but it is illogical to expect long spikes and large flowers from habitually small bulbs.

27

# Temperature and
# Flowering

Distortion of flowers is caused by several things, but the most frequent of these is overheating. While temperature control is not impossible, frequently growers are caught unprepared by a sudden hot day, in which case little can be done. Late-flowering plants are more likely to be the victims than early to mid-season, but the twisting and reflexing of the sepals and petals is less likely to occur in a well-ventilated and shaded glass-house than in open conditions.

Lack of size in the flowers usually indicates poor culture if it occurs on a mature plant, or even on smaller plants. Poor root condition, incomplete fertilising programs, poor watering techniques which allow the plants to dehydrate at a critical stage of bud development, and even incorrect shading are some of the things to guard against.

Color is one of the hardest factors to get right in flowers because it is controlled to a large degree by the prevailing weather at the time the spike forms and develops. However, good positioning relative to the light source can still do a lot for color. This is a good argument for shifting the plants about.

While it is easy to recommend absolute temperature limits, it is difficult sometimes to create them. Mostly it is idealism, but best approached with the idea of getting somewhere near the mark and not leaving it all to nature. In moderate climates it is reasonable to expect a cymbidium to flower its ultimate best once in every four or five years. It is too much to expect it to happen every year, even if several plants of a good clone are grown. Each one will usually be different.

The temperature range for first-quality flowering is rather broad, but the ideal to aim for would be from 16 to 21 degrees Celsius (60 to 70 degrees Fahrenheit). Above that temperature there is a distinct possibility that the petals and sepals will furl the edges and reflex after or during opening stages. If spikes open in widely fluctuating temperatures the flowers will be most uneven in quality and their color altered. The first buds to open should be those about the middle of the spike, closely followed by those above and below, with the tip usually last. If the spike opens in this fashion it will be consistently sized and colored.

In general the spike should completely open in about four days. That is about the ideal period and there could be a difference of as much as 2 centimetres in flower diameter between opening and setting, and an increase of up to 1 centimetre in petal, sepal and dorsal width. All those things happening would indicate that the grower was as nearly well equipped as would be possible. Some growers are fortunate because the climate needs no modification to give results. Others, not so fortunate, may at times have to be content with second best, which at that is not all so bad.

There is no way advice can be given about growing cymbidiums as house plants or in sunrooms. It has been done in isolated instances but remains uncommon. Orchids have been grown indoors as well as in cellars with artificial lighting and heating and all the necessities of life laid on. But generally they are genera other than cymbidiums and the results in all instances are inferior to those gained by planning an outdoor development.

Probably the best way to end this section on environment is to outline and reiterate some of the conditions which will help.

'Guinea-pigging' is an old term used for describing experimental work. It is applicable to orchid growing and a cheap cymbidium plant which will flower is a good way of carrying out a test to see if they are possible in whatever you have to offer. Sometimes these cheap plants are virus-infected, but even these may be used in this way and later consigned to their right place in the incinerator.

Too frequently prospective growers are discouraged and forced out of orchid growing by lack of success. Mostly they get out too soon and should do so only when they are certain it is the environment which is against the project and not their personal efforts. Wildly fluctuating temperatures are against good orchid growing. If this is the problem there are always simple ways of cancelling out and balancing the worst of this feature. Troubled areas are those which are hot and dry through the period of cymbidium growth, October to March. Some humidifying and cooling is indicated. The same area is just as likely to be cold in the flowering period, when some simple form of heating or protection will be needed.

Never stand plants taken indoors in a dish containing water. Any indoor plant needs something to stand on, but instead of the risk of a pool of water forming, fill a dish with coarse gravel, screenings or charcoal and stand the plant on that. The dish of gravel or other material will hold enough water to create a small amount of humidity, which will benefit the plant.

Cymbidiums need to mature into a certain sized plant before they will flower. No rules can be laid down for this size as maturity for one clone may be three mature bulbs and for another a potful, however large the pot may be.

The aspect toward which a plant faces is important. It should be east to north, never west to south.

Some cymbidiums will not grow as well in one area as another, or even in a different glass-house in the same area. The same thing is true of the various colors, which may be grown to a better intensity in different places. Greens for the cooler places, pinks and reds for the warmer ones. But color is not always a good indicator of this phase.

It is not a good idea to buy expensive clones if the plants are to be grown outdoors except if living in an area where cymbidiums are almost naturally growing plants. Choose some of the harder, more durable types, of which there are many. South of latitude 38, cymbidiums as open-air, outdoor cultivated plants are chancy. However, in all states and countries there are small pockets of congenial climate where it is possible. I happen to live in one of these.

Finally, it is possible to go against nature and grow almost anything anywhere, but the ancillary equipment can be so expensive and uneconomic that, if you are a small grower, it is better to settle for something within your scope; it is to you this book is directed as well as to the larger cultivators of the genus.

at times carrying up to twenty or more flowers. The natural habit of the spikes is pendant and they warp and twist when tied erect. This habit is also partly responsible for the trait in hybrids when the spikes are growing or are tied erect. Various reasons are given for this bad habit, but this is the most probable explanation. This cymbidium grows in the Himalayan foothills at altitudes up to 1500 metres and more. It also occurs in other parts of Indo-Asia.

The influence of *Cymbidium lowianum* is persistent, as much of the red in the labellums of hybrids is the *Cymbidium lowianum* feature elaborated and expanded. It also has the effect of averaging out the single flowers of the *eburneum* strain into an acceptable number

*Cymbidium lowianum* has typical cymbidium features such as tall, compressed pseudo-bulbs, the leaves long and sometimes fairly broad and fanning out from the pseudo-bulbs. The flower spikes usually appear on the fully formed pseudo-bulbs in their second year and not on the new leads. But these bulbs will occasionally flower twice in consecutive years, and this influence sometimes reaches out into the hybrid line.

While it is difficult to pinpoint shy flowering characteristics of some hybrids, the fault could scarcely be ascribed to *Cymbidium lowianum,* as it is most free flowering. Unlike the species *eburneum,* it is fairly local in habitat, which has induced speculation that it could be a comparatively recently created species. The word 'recently' could be taken to mean a short while ago, but in the context of species development it could be of the order of some thousands of years. This form of speculation is a very stimulating exercise and one which in most instances is best left in the guesswork stage.

*Cymbidium lowianum* was used by Messrs Theodore Pauwels and Co. of Belgium, with the species *Cymbidium insigne* to produce *Cymbidium* Pauwelsii, a most vigorous and colorful primary hybrid, noted for its immense spikes, which occasionally carried up to thirty flowers quite easily. Several clones of *Cymbidium* Pauwelsii were true tetraploids, but whether natural or induced is unknown. These tetraploids were used in the production of the famous *Cymbidium* Swallows in the early years of tetraploid hybridising, which later extended into the *Cymbidium* Nam Khans and other beautiful hybrids.

*Cymbidium lowianum* flowers are most durable and few hybrids will last as long. This characteristic was recognised almost as soon as it was brought into cultivation and the author Lewis Castle, writing somewhere about 1887, instanced a plant as follows: '*Cymbidium lowianum* ... affords an extraordinary instance of durability, for a fine specimen in Mr. Cobb's garden, Silverdale Lodge, Sydenham, in 1883 opened its flowers on December 26th and the same plant was shown in excellent condition at the Royal Botanic Society's Show, June 18, 1884.'

Perhaps we should add to the quotation that the gardeners who looked after the orchid collections in England put time and thoroughness into cultivation. They were expert yet humble.


*CYMBIDIUM GIGANTEUM,* according to Paxton's Botanical Dictionary, was discovered in Nepal, India, about 1837 and was one of the first of the genus to be brought into cultivation. It also grows in Sikkim, an adjacent province in the Himalayan foothills, as a terrestrial orchid in masses of decaying leaves and as an epiphyte on large evergreen trees. It is usually found in the sub-tropical zone at about 750 to 1500 metres.

In Lindley's *Sertum Orchidaceum,* published first about 1838, its discovery is attributed to Dr Wallich in 1821. The Honourable Court of Directors of the East India Company supplied the material which John Lindley used and he surmised from it that the spike was erect. As we know, the spike is semi-erect and while the color in the illustration shows as red-brown, it should be remembered that Lindley's material was a dried specimen. The color in most instances is basically pale green to yellow-green with sometimes heavy markings of red-brown. As some will remember, there was a clone grown in Sydney in the 1930 period which was almost totally rusty red. The labellum is also marked with red-brown.

The spike usually carries about seven to ten flowers, very durable and tough. The pseudo-bulbs of some clones of *Cymbidium giganteum* are of immense size, egg-shaped and not quite as flattened as those of *Cymbidium tracyanum* or *Cymbidium lowianum*. The leaves of some varieties are short and erect, again unlike those of some of the other species.

The breeding potential of *Cymbidium giganteum* was soon exhausted, as few of its progeny were taken beyond the primary hybrid stage. However, it has the distinction of being one of the parents of the much disputed Phaiocymbidium Chardwarense. *Cymbidium giganteum* may have been discarded too soon, perhaps because it was overshadowed by *Cymbidium i' ansonii*.

*Cymbidium giganteum* is not an easy orchid to flower in cultivation, although it grows well and propagates easily from any division. It is associated with other cymbidiums in a close-knit group occupying the same habitat. This leads to the old guessing game of which came first, the chicken or the egg? Was it *Cymbidium lowianum* or *Cymbidium giganteum*? Or perhaps we have a whole nest of eggs. In common with all the other species cymbidiums, *giganteum* almost dropped out of cultivation and orchid literature after about 1939, when all the breeding and hybridising was overtaken by the introduction of completely new types, a feature of the cult that occurred again about 1960.

*Cymbidium giganteum* flowers on mature pseudo-bulbs, but may occasionally produce a spike on a newly formed growth.

*CYMBIDIUM TRACYANUM* was discovered and brought into cultivation after *Cymbidium giganteum* and was at first mistaken for a larger form of that orchid. It was included in Johnson's Botanical Dictionary of 1917 as *Cymbidium grandiflorum* var. *tracyanum,* which was an obvious mistake.

*Cymbidium tracyanum* grows in the same general area of Asia as *Cymbidium lowianum* and *Cymbidium giganteum,* all members of the large-flowered species. The pseudo-bulbs of *Cymbidium tracyanum,* however, are different from those of the other two and produce longer spikes of larger flowers than *Cymbidium giganteum*. They are also more colorful. The dorsal sepal of *Cymbidium tracyanum* is very hooded over the labellum and column, the flowers frequently talon-like.

First flowered about 1888 in the collection of Mr Tracy, this cymbidium was brought into England with a consignment of *Cymbidium lowianum*. The flowers are pale green to cream basically, sometimes quite golden yellow, but heavily overlaid with blotching and lining of dark purple-brown tones. Well spaced on arching, semi-erect spikes, each flower on a good stem, it is among the earliest of the cultivated species to flower, often opening in May. In cooler seasons or climates they may not open until June. The large spotted and blotched labellum is quite hairy on the central lobe and it has a strong fragrance — to some people a 'smell'. This fragrance is inherent in primary hybrids like *Cymbidium* Doris but seemed to disappear in secondary hybrids.

Many of the *Cymbidium tracyanum* hybrids with later flowering species have mixed flowering periods, but it is most unusual for the early flowering characteristics of *Cymbidium tracyanum* to come out in its hybrids. It is also common to find that its hybrids, like *Cymbidium tracyanum* itself, have somewhat poor lasting qualities as cut flowers. The marked hooding of the dorsal sepal over the labellum and column could indicate that in its habitat the wet season is not ended when the flowers start to open.

One of the few authentic seed counts recorded for species cymbidiums was of approximately 850 000 seeds in one ripened capsule or pod from a self-pollinated flower of *Cymbidium tracyanum,* which is one of the largest of the cymbidium species. It always flowers on the newly forming pseudo-bulb, the spike frequently appearing as early as the end of January in the southern hemisphere.

*CYMBIDIUM GRANDIFLORUM* (synonym *HOOKERANUM*) is again a northern Indian species with distinctive foliage compared with some of the other species. It is markedly striped in light and dark green down the long leaves, particularly at the base. The green flowers are well spaced on long spikes and also on long stems like *Cymbidium lowianum*. The labellum is cream colored with speckling and blotching of red-brown, the same markings extending to the column, the base of the petals and faintly and sparsely on the tips of petals.

*Cymbidium grandiflorum* was brought into cultivation about 1865. It originated in Nepal and other provinces of northern India at elevations of about 1500 to 1800 metres. Growing in oak forest country, it is deluged with rain in the months June to September; from then on to late December the climate is almost dry. It flowers in that period, which would convert to April-May in the southern hemisphere. It may flower later than that in Australia. In its habitat its flowering season would be in the coldest part of the year.

Perhaps the best description of this cymbidium's habitat was recorded in a paper delivered to the Fourth World Orchid Conference in Singapore in 1963 by K. C. Pradhan: 'The sub-temperate zone extends from 5500 feet to 8000 feet and is characterised by gigantic age-old virgin moss-draped forests of oaks, walnut, laurels, michelias, magnolias and echinocarpus, which in the higher regions have reached their prime and since over-matured and turned hollow, harboring masses of *Cymbidium grandiflorum*, *C. elegans*, *C. longifolium*, *C. devonianum*, *C. gammieanum*, *Coelogyne corymbosa*, *Coelogyne occultata* and *Coelogyne ochracea* on their much leaf-littered and rotted hollows.' What followed in this paper was most depressing: '... The rapid development of the country has caught the eyes of the foresters to this uneconomic, over-matured forest and acres and acres of this virgin zone are being cut and burnt annually to fill with other quick-growing, economic species of forest crop. In the process the masses of age-old orchids are being wiped out.'

The parallel to that desecration is occurring in Australia to the last detail. So far as I am concerned I publicise this outrage at every opportunity and seek every means to recruit the orchid-growing and orchid-loving people of this country to fight it.

However, to get back to the story, it will be appreciated from that description of the habitat of *Cymbidium grandiflorum* that it is a cold-growing species and unless some way is found to partly duplicate its environment the orchid will be hard to grow and much more difficult to flower.

*Cymbidium grandiflorum* transmits its clear green color to hybrids many times removed from it, also the beautiful spotting and marking of the labellum and some hybrids, notably *Cymbidium* Cygnus 'Opalescent', have even a beautiful elaboration of the petal-tip spots.

In combination with the monochrome forms of *Cymbidium lowianum*, *Cymbidium grandiflorum* is the base for most of the pure-color yellow and green cymbidiums being produced. *Cymbidium grandiflorum* also projects into some of the hybrids a most undesirable habit of yellowing and casting the buds if the temperature rises above about 18 degrees. High humidity associated with these temperatures will cause it much sooner. This feature comes out most unexpectedly in hybrid productions and unless the pedigree is examined, it may be puzzling. Any infusion of *Cymbidium grandiflorum* breeding, even back to the primary hybrid *Cymbidium* Lowio-grandiflorum could be held responsible if bud-drop occurs.

*Cymbidium grandiflorum* flowers are as large as those of *Cymbidium tracyanum* and the spike is totally pendant from the time it leaves the side of the pseudo-bulb. If any attempt is made to tie it erect it will twist and contort, but it may be held out parallel with the bench or the ground, depending where it is grown, and it will grow straight out. Unfortunately, it does not carry well with this sort of training and if it is to be exhibited it must be erected before the flowers open, otherwise the flowers appear at strange angles when it is tied too late. The spikes usually appear on fully formed pseudo-bulbs, but occasionally also on half-formed growths. If the bases of the pseudo-bulbs are buried too deeply the spikes may abort when they reach the side of the pot or container.

*CYMBIDIUM INSIGNE.* While all the species have separate characteristics, this cymbidium has perhaps more than its share and contributed them to future generations. It was found by Micholitz, in what we now know as Vietnam, about the same time as *Cymbidium erythrostylum* at the beginning of the century. Originally known as *Cymbidium sanderi* in England, where it was flowered by Sanders, the priority of the name *insigne* was established and the form used by Sanders was given the varietal name *sanderi*.

This confusion of species names occurred frequently over the period collectors sent material from the habitat. After collection it was sent variously to England and parts of Europe and classified at the various herbariums and named. One would give the same species a name different from that of another. After search and negotiation the priority was established and the later names used as synonyms in many instances. In some instances the wrangling continues, although that may be a somewhat harsh word with which to describe the negotiations.

*Cymbidium insigne* grows in various areas of Vietnam — or perhaps we should say 'grew', following the American defoliation and destruction in areas of that country, the depredations of collectors, and conversion of so much of the country to cash-cropping and farming. Probably little now remains.

It supplied a section of the color breakthrough in the hybrids and left its mark morphologically with its more rounded pseudo-bulbs, long and rather narrow leaves and erect spikes with most of the flowers on the final arching tip. The flowers are predominantly white to pale pink with deeper shading and lining on the labellum and the interior of the labellum. The bases of the petals and sepals and the column also have red infusions. The labellum is rounded, with two bright gold keels and a gold splash on the front lobe, which is spotted with darker red.

*Cymbidium insigne* is a variable orchid and grows in a higher temperature than many other species. In all, it is a most attractive cymbidium, lacking a little substance in the flower parts, with many admirable characteristics, but seldom seen in cultivation. The flower spikes may appear on new growths as well as older pseudo-bulbs and the climate influencing its maturity seems to have some effect on this.

Some idea of its habitat may be gained from a letter written by Micholitz from Dalat, Cochin China (now Vietnam), to Fred Sander and reprinted in *The Orchid Review* (England) by David Sander: 'Two hundred *insignes* were growing in a little hollow not 100 yards square, water flowing through a regular little bog filled with sphagnum, ferns and clumps of grass lightly shaded by a few pine trees. In this bog the plants had been luxuriating in one huge patch — in full flower — a magnificent sight — the flower spikes of some over six feet high.' Micholitz further confirmed *Cymbidium insigne* as 'essentially a bog plant', but it also grew well in red clay and black soil; 'black mud and fern roots — a most disagreeable job cleaning these plants.' And another footnote, 'they are subject to frost.'

In a further letter on 15 March 1911, Micholitz states that he has 'collected 8000 plants, together with 6500 watsonias, 50 mooreanas and 50 lawrenceanas, 100 parishii Sanderae ... and have got 200 men to carry them to the foothills some 50 kilometres away.' David Sander adds: 'It is sad to think that with that lot he had literally cleared out the area' and pointed out that if more were wanted Micholitz would have to seek a new habitat.

Dalat is 492 kilometres north-east of Saigon and 88.5 kilometres north-west of Phan Rang, on the coast of what is now South Vietnam.

*CYMBIDIUM ERYTHROSTYLUM* was a comparatively late arrival in the orchid houses of England and Europe. It originated in Indo-China, now known as Vietnam. It could perhaps be a form of *eburneum* which has become ecologically and environmentally adapted to this area, as it flowers some three months earlier than *Cymbidium eburneum*. Although white like *Cymbidium eburneum*, *Cymbidium erythrostylum* has up to six and more flowers, the petals projecting forward in a most unwanted way for breeding commercial type flowers or exhibition flowers. Many of the miniature species have this habit. Its early flowering habit has prompted experimental breeding, however, and it has been broken out of the forward thrusting petal habit in many of the fourth and fifth generation hybrids.

Some botanists relate it to both *Cymbidium eburneum* and some of the white flowered miniature species which grow in this part of Asia. The flowers are about the same size as *Cymbidium eburneum,* the labellum creamy with red spotting, blotching, lining or solid color, the column red and the red spotting frequently appearing on the base of the petals and sepals.

Sanders used *erythrostylum* considerably in hybridising and a notable clone imported into Australia was *Cymbidium* Atlantes made by using *Cymbidium* Alexanderi 'Westonbirt'. It was one of the first early-flowering Westonbirt types. Another which came from Sanders was *Cymbidium* Charm 'Elegance' (*Cymbidium* Ceres x *Cymbidium erythrostylum*). The authenticity of this import was frequently challenged, as some authorities maintained that its correct name was *Cymbidium* Sunrise. However, *Cymbidium* Charm was always one of the first cymbidiums to flower in their season and it still appears occasionally, usually without a label and with a query as to its identity. Not too many recognise it.

*Cymbidium* Charm 'Elegance' produced some very dark plum-colored hybrids in its turn, notable among them being *Cymbidium* Andrew Persson, named after one of the early cymbidium hybridists in Australia. *Cymbidium* Charm was a dusky purple-red in good hands, but was frequently called 'dirty' by those to whom it was too much of a challenge. All trace of *Cymbidium erythrostylum* disappeared even in *Cymbidium* Andrew Persson.

*Cymbidium erythrostylum* was discovered by Sanders' collector Micholitz and first flowered for them in 1905. Micholitz was a ruthless collector and, with others, completely obliterated species in many areas of what we now call South-East Asia. It was once known as the Far East. To Micholitz and all orchid seekers and exploiters the world was their 'oyster' and they devoured it.

*CYMBIDIUM I'ANSONII* always seems to be shrugged off as a species of little importance, but nothing could be further from the truth. Its importance is perhaps a matter for chagrin if one reads the foreword by Sir Jeremiah Colman to the first volume of *Sander's List of Orchid Hybrids*.

*Cymbidium i'ansonii* was imported by Hugh Low and Co. in a parcel of plants of *Cymbidium tracyanum* from upper Burma. It was freely suggested at the time that *Cymbidium tracyanum* was a natural hybrid between cymbidiums *lowianum* and *grandiflorum,* but R. A. Rolfe, editor of *The Orchid Review* and a prominent botanist in the orchid world, was not convinced of this on a basic analysis of the flowers of the three cymbidiums. However, in 1900, Rolfe described *Cymbidium i'ansonii* as morphologically similar to *Cymbidium lowianum* and expressed the opinion that it was a hybrid between *Cymbidium lowianum* and *Cymbidium tracyanum,* although that view was not generally held.

As an addition to the range of cymbidium species *Cymbidium i'ansonii* was probably one of the most contentious. It was named after Mr G. I'Anson, one of Hugh Low and Co.'s assistants.

Mr Rolfe later changed his mind about the antecedents of *Cymbidium i'ansonii* and he was not alone in this. It is still something of a mystery because of its comparative scarcity among the thousands of plants of the Indo-Asian cymbidiums imported into England and Europe in those years.

In 1906 a black-and-white illustration of a flower of *Cymbidium i'ansonii* was published in *The Orchid Review,* together with a color description as a light buff-yellow base color with purple-brown veining and with a red-brown median line and red-brown markings on the cream labellum. The original plant passed into the possession of Sir F. Wigan, while other plants subsequently came to light in importations of *Cymbidium tracyanum,* including some found by Dr Alexander Kerr at Chengmai, Siam (now Thailand).

Rolfe's supposed origin of *Cymbidium i'ansonii* was not borne out later by hybridising of the proposed parents. A plant known as *Cymbidium* Mandaianum was exhibited by W. A. Manda, of St Albans, in 1912 and it was indistinguishable from *Cymbidium i'ansonii.* The following year, in April, a plant in flower originating in Annam (now Vietnam) was exhibited by Sanders. It also was similar to *Cymbidium i'ansonii.* In April 1914, W. B. Hartland of Cork, Ireland, exhibited a similar plant named *Cymbidium* Mandaianum, but on this occasion a plant in flower of the cross-pollination of cymbidiums *tracyanum* and *lowianum* was exhibited next to it. The two were totally different. Other plants were also flowered which negated the supposed antecedents of *Cymbidium i'ansonii* as *Cymbidiums tracyanum* and *lowianum.*

To confuse the history further, in 1906 Mr J. W. Moore of Leeds exhibited a hybrid between these two parents under the name of *Cymbidium* Gravenianum. Some thirteen months later, in 1908, an Award of Merit was given to *Cymbidium* Gattonense, derived from the same parentage by Sir Jeremiah Colman, who in deference to opinions of the time changed his name to *Cymbidium i'ansonii* and later parted with propagations of this orchid. He tells the rest of the story in Volume 1 of *Sanders List of Orchid Hybrids.* A few months later another hybrid similarly derived was exhibited by Sir George Holford and in the same year another plant flowered in the collection of W. Bolton. None resembled *Cymbidium i'ansonii* and the natural hybrid theory based on these two parents collapsed.

*Cymbidium i'ansonii* is one of the parents of *Cymbidium* Ceres, with *Cymbidium insigne* the other. Unfortunately, this important hybrid seems to have almost dropped out of cultivation, but it is almost certainly possible that it will have to reappear in the now attenuated pedigree line of the red cymbidium hybrids. *Cymbidium* Ceres was the background to early color lines such as the Carisbrooks, Spartan Queens and later to some of the best red cymbidiums in cultivation, such as the bright clones of *Cymbidium* Sensation.

*Cymbidium* Ceres in some clones had tremendous flower spikes and great vigor, carrying up to twenty flowers well spaced on the racemes. Some featured the white border around the petals and sepals which marks some of the best colored flowers of the 1970-80 period and this bordering is a feature of the species *Cymbidium giganteum* in some of the redder colored clones. This supports the theory still held by some who know the genus that *Cymbidium giganteum* rather than *Cymbidium tracyanum* was the missing link which combined with *Cymbidium lowianum* to produce the natural hybrid *Cymbidium i'ansonii.*

The puzzle about its appearance with parcels of *Cymbidium tracyanum* plants remains one of the unsolved remnants of its history. *Cymbidium i'ansonii* is still cultivated but is seldom seen on exhibition. A Sydney grower of the 1940-50 period named Swinnerton had the last large plant in that city. It grew in an upended 35 centimetre drainpipe and carried about eight or ten spikes of flower, each with some fifteen-odd blooms as I remember it.

Because so much of the species material in the Indo-Asian area has been lost or destroyed over the last century, it is probable that some phases of species orchid occurrence and the development of new types from them is lost for all time. But *Cymbidium i'ansonii* should be remembered for its importance in the color line of many of the ultimate hybrids developed. Its impact was no less than any of the other cymbidium species. Perhaps the final irony of the whole thing is that if reverse cross-pollinations had been made at the time with the original parents we may have had a completely different picture.

*CYMBIDIUM SCHRODERI* was discovered in Annam (Vietnam) about the same time as *Cymbidium insigne* and is in some ways an important species from the hybridists' point of view. It is similar to *Cymbidium giganteum*; pale green to cream basically and striped and blotched, lined and dotted in red to red-brown over the pale background. It is smaller than *Cymbidium giganteum* and again is indicative of the fine line separating nominal species from nominal natural hybrids. The best view is that it is a 'recent' addition to the basic orchid species.

In turn, *Cymbidium schroderi* is the accepted or proposed parent of at least two further additions to the 'recent' species of the area. To solve the question we must get down to such fine points as the natural occurrence or emergence of hybrids all the time in nature, the time span of which is rather more than the insignificant span of a person's life. Extending species listing to *Cymbidium i'ansonii*, and to all other naturally occurring orchids, regardless of the origin, how long they have occupied a habitat, or how few clones there may be, is involved. Perhaps that is one of the more extensive faults of the cult generally — being too involved in hybridising and classifying the product in the light of taxonomy rather than reality. The time involved could be better spent in conserving what little is left of the species.

However, we have been sidetracked again. *Cymbidium schroderi* and *Cymbidium insigne* formed a minor complex of such species. Among them is *Cymbidium cooperi*, introduced from Vietnam with plants of *Cymbidium insigne*. Although more robust than *Cymbidium insigne*, according to Sanders, when it flowered it was thought to be a completely new species. Not long afterwards it was found to resemble in all respects the horticultural hybrid *Cymbidium* J. Davis, raised and flowered by J. Gurney Fowler of England, who used as parents cymbidiums *insigne* and *schroderi*. *Cymbidium cooperi*, therefore, was regarded as a natural hybrid between the two, which was not such a wild flight of imagination as some supposed at the time. At the risk of monotony, we have again a 'whole nest of eggs'; a thought prompted more strongly as all the cymbidium species are taken apart and looked at from a wider viewpoint.

The relative importance of *Cymbidium schroderi* should not be underestimated, nor that of its proposed further hybrids *Cymbidium* J. Davis and *Cymbidium cooperi*.

Again in a consignment of *Cymbidium insigne* sent to England by a collector, another supposed natural hybrid came to light; *Cymbidium roseum*. It should not be confused with the Javanese species of that name. *Cymbidium roseum* was first flowered and exhibited as *Cymbidium glebelandense* var. *roseum*, but is now considered a natural hybrid, probably derived from a back-cross of *Cymbidium cooperi* with *Cymbidium schroderi*. It further confused the register, but is still not accepted by some as originating from this source.

It appears that these three hybrids, *Cymbidiums cooperi, roseum* or *glebelandense* and J. Davis have so much in common that they should be considered an entity. As *Sanders List of Orchid Hybrids* exercises so much latent control over that and as they are listed in that register as J. Davis (*Cymbidium insigne* x *Cymbidium schroderi*), *roseum* (parentage unknown) and *cooperi* (natural hybrid, Sanders) and each has hybrids stemming from them registered in the list, they are separated for all time.

*CYMBIDIUM MAVIS*, also imported from Vietnam with *Cymbidium insigne*, is so much a part of that complex that it has been disregarded as a separate species or natural hybrid, although it appears frequently in early literature associated with the genus.

*CYMBIDIUM RUBY* is another probable natural hybrid which must remain something of a puzzle. It is thought to have originated from *Cymbidium giganteum* and as it appears as a parent in some important breeding lines in the register, notably *Cymbidium* Rio Rita and *Cymbidium* Kanga, its place is assured among the species notables. Its color is indicated by its name and beyond doubt in the two hybrids noted in this paragraph.

Each genus in the Sanders list has some critical gaps, even cymbidiums. Although some probable solutions are offered by cross-check hybrids, there are always 'stirrers' — a horrible word — who, mostly from a sense of rightness, throw doubt on the opinion of others. At times they also cause confusion by their insistence. Research sometimes adds to the confusion owing to the various 'authorities' who insist that they are right or who express divergent lines of thought. As long as mankind continues to cultivate orchids and they remain part of the environment, 'new' ones will continue to appear, filling out further the process responsible for all those cymbidiums collectors have found in the past and sent to various parts of the world. Always provided, of course, that the species continue to find habitats in which to grow.

## Miniatures

Only in the late years of the 1900-80 period was much time given to breeding and cultivating miniature cymbidiums. They were not new things in cymbidium hybridising, as one of the earliest, named Dingleden (*Cymbidium* Alexanderi x *Cymbidium devonianum*), was raised and flowered in the early 1930 period. The project appeared to end there for some time. It is hard to put forward a reasonable explanation for the resurgence of interest, but a hard-headed guess would put it down to diversification in a period which demanded that sort of thing, added to by a flood of orthodox type cymbidiums and the need to create some new line on the sales pitch.

Originally these miniatures followed the line of true miniature plants, with miniature flowers, bred from species like *pumilum* cross-pollinated with larger, normal cymbidiums. But the plan was confused by an influx of so-called polymins and flowers that were neither one thing nor the other. Many of these are now termed novelty cymbidiums as distinct from miniatures, because of size restrictions. A large number of the polymins and miniatures look remarkably like culls from the period following the introduction of the Westonbirt strain.

Some of the true miniatures bred from the species *Cymbidium pumilum;* cymbidiums *suave, madidum, canaliculatum* or *Cymbidium devonianum* and others could not be produced in sufficient numbers to satisfy the initial demand, and there were never enough propagations of beautiful miniatures like *Cymbidium* Olymilum to satisfy the market. Most of these true miniatures were correctly named, for morphologically they conformed to the description, whereas at times the foliage of plants which produced small flowers and were called miniatures was longer, wider and stronger than many of the orthodox cymbidiums. The possibility of producing cymbidiums for warmer climates from some of the small cymbidium bloodlines is possible, also plants which will flower through the normal out-of-season dead time of a normal cymbidium collection. Some of the miniature species are as follows:

*CYMBIDIUM DEVONIANUM* deserves pride of place in the list since it was probably one of the first parents of the breed in conjunction with an unknown form of *Cymbidium* Alexanderi. It is a native of northern India, originally brought into cultivation about 1837 and named in honor of the Duke of Devonshire, one of the early growers. Base color in the flowers is light green on which are superimposed small spots of crimson to brown over almost the whole of the flower. The labellum is also light green with pronounced spotting and blotching of deep purple-crimson. The color is variable but basically the same in the varieties used for miniature hybridising.

*CYMBIDIUM PUMILUM* is probably the most important of the species used. It is native to southern China, Japan and rarely in other places. Although there are many colored forms, the type most used is the albino or pale green form, and it has produced some notable hybrids when used with normal cymbidiums.

The Australian cymbidiums are among the smallest of the genus florally; one is among the largest morphologically (*Cymbidium madidum*), one has possibly the most unusual foliage of any cymbidium, and the third resembles *eburneum* in its plant habit.

*CYMBIDIUM MADIDUM* has blurred habitat boundaries, but generally speaking greatest numbers occur between Newcastle, New South Wales, and the central portion of Queensland coastal areas. It is found in semi-tropical, moist forest areas, frequently growing in aged and dead staghorn and elkhorn masses on the trunks of trees. Some plants are beyond belief in size. One such, growing in a dead staghorn and removed from a tree in the coastal area near Grafton, New South Wales, provided several large plants to the collector and the detritus left behind included almost a wheelbarrow full of back-bulbs. *Cymbidium madidum* has the smallest flowers of the Australian

Miniature cymbidiums became popular much later than standard size flowers and come from different species than their larger relatives.

section, well spaced out on a fairly long raceme which is totally pendant. The color is green-yellow, even to the labellum, which has a red to purple-red blotch on the central lobe. It is not an easy species to cultivate and dislikes humid conditions at certain times during its annual cycle, particularly in the cooler months of the year.

*CYMBIDIUM SUAVE* is usually found in decaying sections of eucalypts, both live and dead. I have seen plants growing in stumps left following felling for timber, in knot-holes left from fallen branches on live trees, in the ends of broken branches and also in forks where the roots can penetrate into the decaying centre of the tree. It is found only where the roots can reach decaying wood and although the plant is morphologically small, with leaves about half a metre long and about 2 centimetres wide, the root system has been known to descend through the centre of a decayed tree for up to 10 metres (about 32 feet). The flower spikes are short, about 33 centimetres long at times, with up to thirty or more flowers on a spike. The flowers are slightly larger than those of *Cymbidium madidum,* about 15 millimetres across, the petals forward jutting similar to those of *madidum* and the color varying from pale green-yellow to spotted with rusty red or red-purple over the surface of the petals and sepals. The labellum is basically green-yellow with a purple-red blotch on the central lobe and extending into the labellum. Like *Cymbidium madidum,* it flowers in September-October.

*CYMBIDIUM CANALICULATUM* is a native of drier Queensland and New South Wales. While the plant is not uncommon morphologically, the foliage more resembles that of some of the oncidiums like *lanceanum* than that of orthodox cymbidiums. It is thick and deeply channelled, almost to the point of being terete. The flowers of *Cymbidium canaliculatum* vary considerably from pale green-yellow base color suffused with minute spotting of red purple and rusty red-brown, to deepest purple-red in the variety *sparkesii.* The flowers are borne on a raceme similar to that of *Cymbidium suave* and like that cymbidium the spikes are semi-pendant to pendant and borne freely, with sometimes three and four spikes on the one pseudo-bulb on well-grown plants. Of the Australian cymbidiums, it probably resents disturbance more than the others. It grows in open forest country and its foliage gives some clue to the type of environment in which it lives — harder than that of either of the others. In the order of harshness of their environments, *Cymbidium madidum* has the softest, *suave* the next, with *canaliculatum* morphologically adapted to sometimes very harsh conditions. It is reported to extend over the whole of the northern Australian sector, east to west, but much of this territory is unexplored botanically. Again, it is epiphytic, living on decaying vegetation and particularly decaying wood.

*CYMBIDIUM SINENSE* (synonym *HOOSAI*) is a native of southern China and Formosa. There are several varieties, including an albino form. The colored forms shade through various tones to deep purple-brown. Over the years, where considerable information has been assembled about the orthodox sized species cymbidiums, that about the miniatures is patchy, with little or no information as to the period of discovery and attention to cultivating them.

*CYMBIDIUM GOERINGII* (synonym *VIRESCENS*), *CYMBIDIUM SUAVISSIMUM* and several other species have been used, but the hybrids emanating from these lesser-used species do not give the numbers appropriate to separate listing and description. For instance, there are sixteen species cymbidium miniatures in the island of Formosa, including *Cymbidium sinense, Cymbidium lancifolium, Cymbidium simonsianum* and *Cymbidium illiberale,* which have been used once or twice in the past and may again be used if worthwhile hybrids appear from them.

As orchids, the miniature cymbidiums have not had much time devoted to them and, in the past, they have been treated as botanical subjects rather than mainstream orchids usually found in collections.

41

# Pollination and Hybridising

The first thing to understand in hybridising or pollinating flowers is the way the flower is constructed and how to use the pollen. In cymbidium flowers the column, which is the solid erect part of the flower above the lip or labellum, carries both the pollen, under a little cap at the tip of the column, and the stigma, which is the cavity immediately underneath the tip. If the cap is gently pushed off with a wooden matchstick the pollen will be visible. Using the same match, the pollen can be picked off with an upward lift under the tip of the column. It will stick to the match. Sometimes it comes off with the cap and must be separated. It is solid, not powdery, and if fresh and usable should be light yellow colored.

If the pollen is pressed up into the cavity under the tip of the column it will stick there and fertilisation of the flower should follow. Pollen can be used on the flower from which it is lifted or it may be used on another flower. The term used to describe the first process is self-pollination and the second is cross-pollination.

The word 'hybridising' really means cross-pollinating two different species or at times different genera. The product from such cross-pollinations is called hybrids. When two different varieties of one species are cross-pollinated the resultant seedlings are known as siblings. They are raised at times to improve species, color, shape or some other feature.

Cymbidium seed pods take up to ten or twelve months at times to ripen and burst. Considering the amount of work involved in sowing and raising the seed, it can be more economically carried out by commercial seed-raising nurseries, who advertise their services in most orchid publications.

There should be good reasons for making cross-pollinations, not just carrying out the process for the fun of it. If it is done, it should follow research and with some knowledge of the chromosome count of the parents. Most pollinations end in failure to set seed or mature a seed pod for a number of reasons. Chromosome count is explained later in this section.

Long ago when the process was started it was simple. The innovators did not really know what they were doing. Let me quote a favorite snippet, written by Dr Lederberg of Stamford University, USA, in relation to hybridising and cross-pollination: 'It is in this century that we have lost the comfort of blind ignorance — we are beginning to use our intelligence to understand what we are doing.' Intelligent hybridising or pollination should be an aim, as the day of the innovator is about over.

But it is always the innovators who seem to have the most fun. They start off with new material and new ideas, sometimes thought out, others at random, and if they are fortunate they come up with something everyone wants. When modern cymbidium hybrids are critically examined it may seem incredible that they came from the original material and the innovators certainly did not know what the results would ultimately be. The innovators, however, had an advantage in the richness of the material. They had the choice of hundreds of varieties of the species from which to select parents, even at times using siblings from selected parents. They could well ask in the late years of the twentieth century: 'What else is the hybridist looking for?'

Cymbidiums have certain genetic limitations as far as size is concerned. The limitations have been circumvented to some degree by introduction of higher chromosome counts and genetic changes. Perhaps in fairness it should be agreed that the quest is for size combined with other attributes, such as color and shape, with a very large emphasis on the size and color of the labellum. The quest for size was a major preoccupation of the 1960-70 decade, but hybridists did not really approach the dimensions of such an early hybrid as Matador, a variety of which had a span of 18 centimetres and more, although with very narrow flower segments. Its breeding was *Cymbidium* Schlegelii x *Cymbidium tracyanum.*

The inherent limitations apply equally to color and what hybridists accomplished in that decade is little more than they did at other periods in cymbidium development. The outstanding feature was amalgamation of color and shape as well as intensification of some colors, such as in *Cymbidium* Sensation. But in some shades of red and pink in clear tones there seems still some way to go.

The best way to describe the work of hybridists over the last forty years in many genera, including cymbidiums, is that they twisted the natural attributes of flowers to satisfy conformity to a set of standards, some of which were unreal, laid down for competitive display or the commercial requirements of flower vendors. Some hybridists may feel aggrieved at that description of their activities, but if so they can always put up an amendment.

A look at these developments shows that cymbidium flowers were created to conform to a set of features demanded by a group of people who allotted some 60 per cent of a total appreciation to two features — color and shape. Number of flowers, positioning on the spike and habit were given a minor role.

Success in this regard was remarkable, because in the first instance the shapely attribute of rounded tips on petals and sepals was almost absent in cymbidium species. One of the first hybrids, *Cymbidium* Eburneo-lowianum (Veitch, 1889), was strongly color influenced by *Cymbidium eburneum,* but the floriferous habit of *Cymbidium lowianum* prevailed as did its morphological characteristics; the pseudobulbs were *lowianum* type and it had strong, wide leaves quite unlike those of *Cymbidium eburneum.* The golden keels and frontal part of the labellum of *Cymbidium eburneum,* however, proved persistent, playing a big part in production of what are termed pure-color hybrids. Hybrids of such distinction as the *Cymbidium* Rosanna line, started about the early 1930 period by Lionel de Rothschild, carry these keels to a marked degree. The smaller number of flowers on spikes is also an inherent factor traceable through breeding lines to *Cymbidium eburneum.* Most growers will recognise the trait in many clones of *Cymbidium* Balkis. Indeed, it is also a strong characteristic of *Cymbidium* Alexanderi 'Westonbirt', one of the all-time greater cymbidiums.

Lacking the techniques now available, too frequently the work on the color intrusions in varieties of *Cymbidium eburneum* and *Cymbidium parishii* led to too few seedlings being raised to test the true potential of the pollinations. While it is too difficult to speculate on what may have emerged, it would be a logical inference that the long drawn-out processes of the 1900-70 period could have been shortened. It would also be an advantage if some of the older material was reworked, allowing for a program extending over some years, so that some of the lost genes could perhaps be recovered and a completely new group of colors found. Much of the original material is doubtless lost, and that is to be deplored, as these plants were selected from thousands of clones imported into both England and Europe and those not measuring up to a standard were subsequently destroyed.

The amalgamation of *Cymbidium eburneum, Cymbidium lowianum* and *Cymbidium grandiflorum* has given hybridists a breeding line from which they are able to breed green cymbidiums at will and reselection of parent plants has shaped these green hybrids into something considered ideal. Orchid growers are hard to satisfy and as soon as the rounded outline of cymbidium flowers had been achieved, some fanciers decided that it was too cupped and the flower should be open yet rounded. A reselection of parents was made and that rounded open outline has been achieved in a fair proportion of the hundreds of thousands of seedlings raised. That proportion was decided long before hybridists began to interfere with nature, but they should even win that battle if past victories in horticulture have any meaning, and we will get to the stage where there is little that has been demanded but not achieved.

In nature it is the habit of orchids and other forms of flowering plants to throw up occasional superb specimens that outshine normal and poor standard flowers. They are key clones and are present in many instances of cattleya hybridising in particular. But it is not the average common in nature and is there solely to break breeding lines, in the same way as the poor flower type is there to break those lines. It is the survival mechanism of all species and it is still present in hybrids. Those species which do not produce variations soon disappear in the natural sort-out which is going on all the time.

It is at this point that the hybridist is in some ways approaching the end of cymbidium breeding. A return to species or primary hybrid level at about the tenth or twelfth generation is needed, and even much sooner in some lines, to impart new vigor and avoid bad morphological characteristics, such as disease susceptibility, bad root systems and poor plant form, which are beginning to show. Some hybridists have already realised this and also the role of tetraploid breeding. The naturally occurring tetraploid is usually a once-only specimen weeded out in the second generation because of breeding incapability. But they still occur, how and why we do not know.

The in-between colored cymbidiums are still lacking certain characteristics. Two lines in this group under development are what are called the non-staining cymbidiums and the clear-color cymbidiums.

Non-staining cymbidium breeders seek to eliminate the darkening of the sepals in the bud stage, so that when the flower opens there is no color on the outside to 'ghost' through to spoil the clearness of the inside surfaces. The staining characteristics are partly cultural and partly inherent and it is clear that while cymbidiums may be non-staining under certain cultural conditions they will stain under others. Breeding may minimise this but, in view of the derivation of cymbidiums from the species concerned, it is doubtful if a complete line can ever be produced.

The clear-color cymbidiums have a part to play in the hybrid production line, but only a part. It is obvious that a total line of clear-color cymbidiums with yellow or monochrome labellums is not wanted. But if by clear color the tints and colors in the petals and sepals are those suggested, then that is a most valuable contribution to the genus. Clear color is what most growers want, and a contrasting labellum is the thing which shows it up.

The monochrome labellum comes mostly from two sources — the combination of the labellum tints of *eburneum* and the monochrome forms of *Cymbidium lowianum* such as the *concolor* variety. Occasionally this is referred to as an albino strain, but the derivation of the word soon indicates that another term is needed.

Clear colors are wanted to satisfy two criteria. First to satisfy judging standards, where a large percentage is awarded for that feature; and second for growers for the export market, which in some instances discount what to most people are beautiful cymbidiums. A lot of the prejudice against striped and colored cymbidiums, however, has faded away.

For the cymbidium grower as such, as against the flower exporter, it is rather foolish to discard cymbidiums because they do not conform to judging standards or for other reasons when they fit very well into a collection. Each of us has preferences and should respect those of others.

That brings in the question of culling or not culling. It seems to be done for two reasons — to upgrade a poor collection, which may have been plants bought for experience or as starters, or to make way for something new and not knowing where to begin at choosing those to be sold or put out.

Upgrading a collection has its limits; do not try to keep abreast of cymbidium hybrid name lists by buying new hybrids on principle or because 'the Joneses' are doing it. All the fun soon goes out of the hobby and you never get the chance to stabilise the collection and flower them at their best. One of the hardest lessons to learn is to be satisfied with a good collection of flowering plants and not try to add every outstanding cymbidium to it as they appear. It pays to remember, too, that what looks good in some other state or collection may not grow as well in any other state or glass-house.

It is easy to pick the plants in collections which represent lost interest for some reason or other and too frequently these plants are the species if they are grown. All cymbidium growers should try to fit in two or three of these into their collections and grow them as they do their more expensive purchases, because they are disappearing at an increasing pace from 'back of beyond'. It is no exaggeration to say that in the near future when the science of horticulture looks for a particular species of cymbidium it will not be there. Science has deduced that each year up to five or more plant species disappear, forever.

# Pollinating a Cymbidium Flower

A simple explanation of the flower construction is that, starting from the top, it has an upper or dorsal sepal, two petals at each side and two lower sepals. The sepals enclose the flower when it is a bud and may discolor in adverse conditions. The central part of the flower comprises two features — the labellum or lip and the column, which combines the sexual parts of the flower, namely the pollen and stigmatic surface, which are unlike those of ordinary annuals or other flowers. The pollen is solid in two masses and the stigmatic surface is a cavity under the tip.

The flower is here cut away to expose the column. The tool used in pollination or cross-pollination from flower to flower is an ordinary wooden toothpick, always discarding it after use and not using it on another pollination.

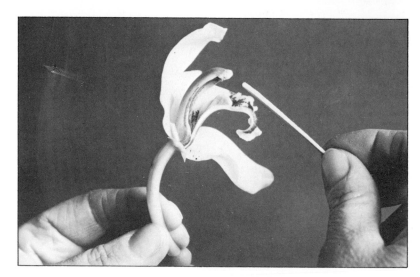

The tip of the columm has a little white cap covering the pollen masses. It is easily dislodged, but if the process is roughly handled the pollen may also come away with it. In this illustration the pollen mass may be easily seen still attached to the end of the column, with the cap on the end of the toothpick. Discard the cap after removing the pollen if it comes away with it.

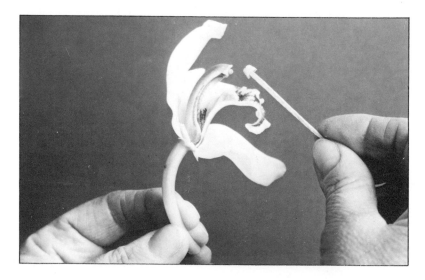

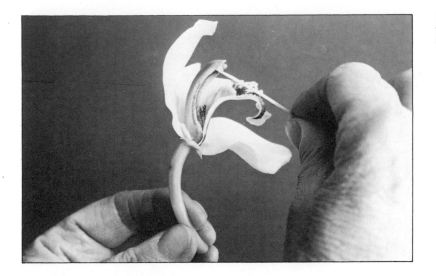

Insert the tip of the toothpick underneath the tip of the column to touch it on the sticky surface of the stigmatic cavity.

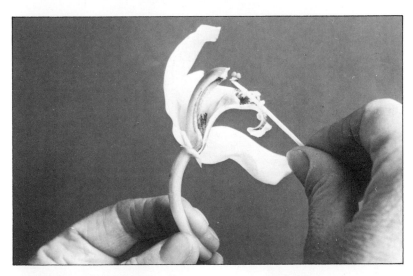

The toothpick or other tool is then drawn gently past the tip of the column and the nodes of pollen will come away cleanly from it.

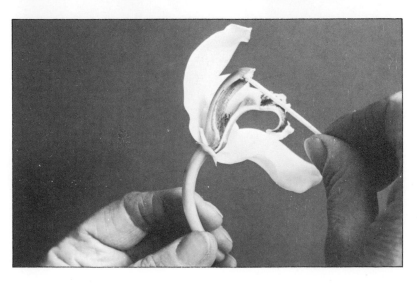

Once attached to the tip of the toothpick, the pollen may then be gently pushed back into the cavity if it is desired to self-pollinate the flower, or it may be transferred to another flower after the pollen mass has been dislodged from it by the same process. Do not leave the pollen on a flower which you may be cross-pollinating, because when the column starts to swell this pollen mass may also be engulfed in the process and give a part self-pollination. If fertile, the seed pod may take up to twelve months to ripen. The raising of the seed is a complicated and expensive process and it is not intended to describe it in this book, as other publications should be consulted for it. Neither should the pollinating process be taken lightly, as there are too many poor cymbidiums grown, without adding to the number. Every cross-pollination should be studied and undertaken with the aim of improving the genus in some way, not merely as a pastime.

Pollinating a paphiopedilum flower is a little more difficult but essentially the same.

Looking at the flower face on, the central portion is occupied by a plate-like boss. On each side of this boss and just below the openings on each side of the pouch or labellum are small horn-like anthers carrying the pollen masses.

On the inside face of this boss is the same sticky surface ready to receive the solid pollen mass if it happens to be dislodged by an insect in the ordinary natural processes as it attempts to enter or leave the pouch.

Deliberate cross-pollination or self-pollination is best effected by carefully cutting away so much of the back of the pouch as to be able to place the pollen on the stigmatic surface, or to press the pouch downward to expose the pollinating surface. Some pollinators prefer to smear the pollen mass on a clean surface first, then transferring the smeared mass to the stigmatic surface. One reason is that occasionally the surface of the pollen mass may be rendered infertile while the inner portion could be clean and fertile.

As with cymbidiums, only trial and error can be given as a guide to the fertility or compatability of one flower to another, but it is also wise to do the reverse cross-pollination at the same time, as the sex-linkage of male or female receptiveness is a well-known if unproven fact in orchid breeding.

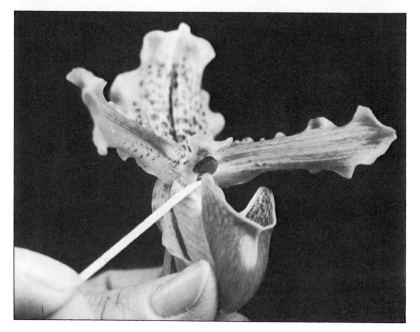

# Classifying by Chromosome Count

What follows is a basic explanation of a complex subject and one which may not interest many cymbidium growers. Most of these people will no doubt have heard of diploids, triploids, tetraploids and polyploids and bypassed them in their minds as being complicated things which do not matter very much in growing cymbidiums. But they are quite simple to understand and do matter very much in selecting and growing these orchids.

Each living thing is made up from minute parts called cells. In each normal cymbidium cell there are forty chromosomes. As parts of the plant, such as the roots, grow the cells divide and form new cells. As each does so the chromosomes also split, with forty parts going into each cell. The new cells are complete forty chromosome cells which rest, grow, and later divide in turn. This is the process by which even we as human beings develop from babies to children to adults.

The chromosomes are in turn composed of minute bodies called genes, and these govern size, color and all the other features which go to make up a cymbidium plant. These plants with forty chromosome cells are called diploids. They are normal in every way. In a fertile or viable diploid seed the pollen finally contributes only twenty chromosomes, the embryo in the ovary twenty chromosomes, so preserving the forty chromosome or diploid status of the seed. This is a simple or casual explanation of a complicated natural process.

In tetraploid cymbidiums a mutation occurs at the first simple growth and division. The first cell does not completely divide and so a double cell with eighty chromosomes is formed. This is perpetuated in all the following cells. It is an unusual process and one which in some instances gives cymbidiums what we like to see — larger flowers and above normal vigor in the plant and breeding processes. However, if a tetraploid is used in hybridising there is no certainty that fertility will result.

A triploid results in most instances where a diploid is cross-pollinated or fertilised by a tetraploid. It is a simple matter of addition and division, triploids having sixty chromosome cells. These triploids may or may not be fertile. That is, they may or may not be capable of forming seeds or carrying fertile pollen.

While these three categories are the regulars, there are others with confused numbers of chromosomes above and below the three categories which are termed polyploids, and these also may be fertile or infertile. The derivation of the words is purely scientific and of little interest to most cymbidium growers, but the actual status of the plants is important.

There is only one sure way in which the categories of cymbidiums can be determined to say they are diploids, triploids, tetraploids, or those which have even larger numbers or odd numbers of chromosomes, and that is by a microscopic chromosome count, usually carried out photographically. There are some other methods used, but they are unreliable and inaccurate, because many of those with irregular or odd numbers of chromosomes over and above diploid status also have the same visual indicators.

Modern cymbidiums, reds, pinks, whites, greens and all the other colors and mixtures, are now the result of scientific knowledge of chromosomes and heredity — a knowledge which could have saved a lot of time in the first place if available. The use to which this knowledge can be put is limited by the capability of buyers to take up the output from the commercial producers of new hybrids or to make room for their own productions.

In all the science available some colors, such as blue, have eluded the hybridist. This is not unusual on analysis of the species. It is probable that there are no genes in the chromosome total for that color. Unless science can inject that factor into the genes, or induce them in some way to produce those genes as the Japanese did with the common Australian budgerigar, the blue cymbidium is likely to remain a dream. By blue the real color is inferred, not what might by some fancy be described as a tint or even a shadow of blue. Also, so far, no hybridist has produced a clear, non-lined red cymbidium. This is in no way belittling their achievements. At least they are some way towards it. The factor must be there in the tangled web of genes in the chromosomes.

Reverting to the species, it was the combination of the *Cymbidium insigne-schroderi* complex with the *i'ansonii* (*Cymbidium giganteum-tracyanum-lowianum*) complex which initiated the red or near-red in the genus. *Cymbidium i'ansonii* cross-pollinated with *Cymbidium insigne* brought *Cymbidium* Ceres. *Cymbidium cooperi*, the *Cymbidium schroderi* affiliate, cross-pollinated with *Cymbidium i'ansonii* brought *Cymbidium* Magali Sander, which in turn led to *Cymbidium* Susette and thence to Lowville, one of the densest of the near-red cymbidiums. *Cymbidium* Sabre Dance and several of the other near-perfect reds should soon bring results, therefore it is not wise to be dogmatic and say a clear red is impossible.

All the reds, despite the beautiful elaborations of the white borders to the petals and sepals and magnificent complementary labellums, still have the fault of lines of different color in the petals and sepals. Perhaps a better description of the flower would be to say it has a base color and add to this base a series of blotches, speckles and lines in red and red-brown which give the overall impression of a red flower. Superb as they are, perhaps we are looking at the best we can do and ask too much from the genes of the species.

*We have only the best shaped of these cross-pollinations of reds and pinks — the badly shaped and colored clones have long since been destroyed, and with them perhaps the genes we have been so eagerly looking for. They lost out on a set of inappropriate standards being imposed on them.*

Probably one of the best scarlet-red cymbidiums ever produced was *Cymbidium* Ceres 'F.J. Hanbury', which, when well grown and flowered, was fiery.

The lining of darker color in many of the green cymbidiums, which was inherited from *Cymbidium lowianum* as much as any other species, is still apparent to plague much of the quest for pure green cymbidiums. But with the green factors for color in so many hybrid lines there is always the chance in cross-pollinations that these green factors will come out intensely instead of as pastel tints. At present it is possible to get white, pink, yellow or green shades in different clones from one cross-pollination. Predictability is by no means as clear as sometimes conveyed in sales talk, although it can always be concluded that the hybridist must be right sometimes.

It could be asked if the flowered clones of any pollination present a true cross-section of the potential. A return to the quoted number of seeds in a pod, as outlined earlier, gives sufficient reason to doubt that in all instances either the best, or even a representative selection, is produced from the minimal sowings and propagations to flowering stage in any one pollination. That could be qualified by, say, a cross-pollination to produce the hybrid *Cymbidium* Joan of Arc (*Cymbidium* Alexanderi 'Westonbirt' x *Cymbidium* Balkis), where it could be predicted with some certainty that the shape, color and labellum patterns would be constant throughout, owing to the inbreeding involved and the fact that the expectation would be for almost a total tetraploid production, allowing for the vagaries of nature and a few non-conformists. The result with any other variety of *Cymbidium* Alexanderi would be far from predictable. Mendel's laws ceased to have much relevance in cymbidium hybridising quite soon after the primary stages.

Reversions, once the bane of the hybridist, no longer seem to occur with the same drastic results. Although still possible in a proportion of seedlings raised from

*Cymbidium* Atlantes was bred as a triploid by cross-pollinating two selected flowers.

cross-pollinations, they could not reach the fantastic color abnormalities or the 5 millimetre wide petals and sepals so common in many of the secondary hybrids of the early days.

The only total potential of cross-pollinations realised are in the instances of so little seed forming in a pod or capsule as to cause the total to be sown, sometimes in one or two flasks. The inability of the plant to produce a good full pod does little to encourage the belief that it is a good cross-pollination, or that the resultant seedlings will in their turn make good parents. Generally the seed from these pods is difficult to germinate and the seedlings hard to raise. They are usually completely out of balance.

In nature it is difficult to say what proportion of the seed in a capsule would germinate and grow to reach flowering size. In hazarding a guess, it would appear from the number of seeds contained in capsules or pods on a bush or naturally growing plant of *Cymbidium madidum,* and the number of plants in the immediate vicinity of the seed-bearing clone which could be counted, that it could be as low as one in 5 000 000. This is, of course, most difficult to verify, as the seed is wind-blown as well as directly dropped. But the comparative scarcity of plants and the number of pods formed on mature plants would seem to back up the estimate, in view of the restrictive nature of the environment and ecology in which it germinates and grows. *Cymbidium suave* would seem to confirm the figure.

If we revert to the description of the environment and numbers of plants growing in the Sikkim forests as described by Pradhan, it should be apparent that there must be a large number of pollinations, formation of capsules and scattering of seed in the area. Little insight is required to estimate that the number of germinations and subsequent establishment of new clones must be as infinitesimally small as that quoted for *Cymbidium madidum,* otherwise there would not now be the problem of possible extinction of the species. The natural environments are strictly limited. On the lighter side, I once remember seeing a germinated and growing single-bulb seedling of *Cymbidium madidum* in a tiny knot-hole on the side of a Banksia tree and often wondered how it was going to make the grade with nothing much to expand or grow in or on.

51

That is part of the answers to the questions at the beginning of the book. Another part lies in the discovery of the breeding potential of *Cymbidium* Alexanderi 'Westonbirt', first flowered in 1911 by Sir George Holford. His orchid grower was Mr H. G. Alexander, who emerges as the paramount figure in all cymbidium history and cultivation. The true value of this cymbidium was not realised until much later, when its use as a parent became more widespread. Weak in foliage, with obvious virus infection, it was later found to be unusual in its genetic make-up, with double the number of chromosomes carried in the normal cymbidium cell.

*Cymbidium* Alexanderi 'Westonbirt' was possibly the first recognised tetraploid, but in hybridising history it was not the only one. *Cymbidium* Pauwelsii 'Comte de Hemptine' was another, also morphologically weak. Other varieties of Pauwelsii were also tetraploids, some distinctly robust in flowering and plant health. I grew and flowered one of them for many years and regarded it as one of the parents of *Cymbidium* Babylon and other notable hybrids on labellum patterns.

In the early years from 1920 to 1940 these Alexanderi hybrids were known as 'Westonbirt strain' and hundreds of superior clones were introduced to Australia in the period just before and during the early stages of the second world war, which put a temporary stop to hybridising and caused the dispersal of the British breeding clones to other countries, including America.

One of the tetraploids which came from *Cymbidium* Alexanderi 'Westonbirt' was *Cymbidium* Rosanna 'Pinkie'. The other parent, *Cymbidium* Kittiwake, apparently also was a chance tetraploid, which could be the reasonable explanation of the chromosome count of *Cymbidium* Rosanna. Not all the Rosannas, however, were potential breeders, some were failures. In turn, *Cymbidium* Rosanna 'Pinkie' was a parent of *Cymbidium* Balkis. This line is a doubtful source for non-staining cymbidiums, as one of their characteristics is definite staining of the sepal backs.

In this bloodline one of the strange twists in *Sanders Orchid Hybrid List* comes to light. *Cymbidium* Dryad and *Cymbidium* Gottianum were the parents of *Cymbidium* Kittiwake. *Cymbidium* Dryad and *Cymbidium* Gottianum are virtually the same thing if the proposed synonymity of *Cymbidium parishii* and *Cymbidium eburneum* is recognised. Both also have the species *Cymbidium insigne* as the common parent on the other side. While this is a reflection on the authority of Sanders hybrid list, and although it is full of other problems in other genera, orchids are far better documented than most plants.

The second and disappointing surprise about breeding with *Cymbidium* Alexanderi 'Westonbirt' and other tetraploids was that the seedlings from normal or diploid clones seemed sterile and most were beautiful cymbidiums. It was an unfortunate end

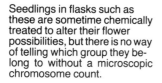

Seedlings in flasks such as these are sometime chemically treated to alter their flower possibilities, but there is no way of telling which group they belong to without a microscopic chromosome count.

to what seemed the starting point for breeding orchids which had a rounded outline as well as rounded tips on petals and sepals.

It seemed a dead-end had been reached, but further search produced more tetraploids. It is possible to have whole collections of these cymbidiums. However, the future of cymbidiums rests with the normal clones and not with tetraploids and other non-conformists, a fact which has been realised by many hybridists.

The simple history of the various phases through which hybridising passed is seen as the original production of normal cymbidiums, the search for better results, then the discovery of the tetraploids, the introduction and discarding of the triploids as breeders, the production of more tetraploids and their use in various ways to produce necessary qualities in the hybrids. By 'necessary' is meant what was or is popular at any given time. Many thousands of cross-pollinations produced discards, with a minority of clones retained. It is essential to know the derivation of prospective cymbidiums to produce further hybrids and time can be saved if pedigrees and varieties used are known for what they are in chromosome count as well as clonal origin.

Colchicine, a plant derivative to change chromosome counts, has been used for very many years and the technique is not too difficult. But it has never been the publicised origin for many cymbidium hybrids in orchid literature. That source of information, however, does record changes in chromosome character of known clones used in propagation.

Occasionally plants are listed as tetraploids when their true chromosome count is not known. Classification by guard cell size is unreliable and unacceptable, as it uses only peculiar leaf abnormalities and not cellular determinations.

Storing pollen to use on later flowering plants has changed some of the early-flowering types which had undesirable characteristics. Anyone can do this, provided the pollen is properly sealed and refrigerated. The general idea of this is to plan a flower crop over a period of nine or ten months which, with artificial lighting, heating, cooling and other controls, is quite possible. Cymbidiums are orchids needing a succession of changes in cultural environment to alter plant processes from growth to flowering and even a partial dormancy. Unless these changes can be artificially created, early-flowering types will always remain early and the late-flowering ones late. Hybridising between the two groups results in transmission of good qualities lacking in the one and early-flowering qualities projected into the other.

Miniature characteristics may not be all that could be wished for, with their forward-jutting petals and small labellums, but the same amount of work given to their improvement as to the larger cymbidiums could soon effect remarkable changes. It would be unrealistic to expect summer flowers to last long, but as these miniatures seem to produce plenty of flower spikes they could be expected in succession.

A long gap followed one of the first registered miniatures, *Cymbidium* Langleyense (*Cymbidium devonianum* x *Cymbidium lowianum*), named about 1911. The next one was *Cymbidium* Dingleden, about 1933, probably followed by *Cymbidium* Minuet (*Cymbidium insigne* x *Cymbidium pumilum*), usually credited to Mr H. G. Alexander, but the cross-pollination was made, it appears, by his son. *Cymbidium* Minuet took the cymbidium world by storm and gained an Award of Merit from the RHS Orchid Committee in 1949. It is still a favorite with many cymbidium growers.

None of these hybrids had both parents as miniatures and that set a pattern followed since, because in most instances the miniatures have been cross-pollinated with orthodox larger cymbidiums. Apparently *Cymbidium* Minuet is sterile, as no further registered hybrids have appeared from it. But the *Cymbidium devonianum* hybrids have been further used, with the beautiful labellum coloring reproduced and intensified.

The obsession with shape remained as an inhibiting characteristic of some of the people adjusting the judging of orchids, and this led to the side-tracking of the original concept of a profusion of flowers on small, freely-produced spikes. One of the pleasing features about this hybridising, however, was production of cymbidiums which seemed able to withstand climates not tolerated by the normal types, provided the parents were selected with that idea in mind. Although there is little chance that these orchids could supplant the genera usually cultivated in semi-tropical areas, they may nevertheless form a beautiful addition to collections in such places.

It took a long time for cymbidium hybridising to get going; up to 1945 there were only some 1150 hybrids registered, compared with over 4500 paphiopedilums and some 2700 laeliocattleyas, without counting the remainder of the cattleya complex.

The early cymbidium hybrids gave no promise of the glittering array, or any real indication of the lengths to which the art of orchid breeding could be taken. Only a minor portion of orchid growers of the 1960s onward would remember the type or color of hybrids available in the years 1920-40, when their hybridising really commenced. Such things as the *Cymbidium* Ceres varieties or their followers, the red and pink *Cymbidium* Carisbrooks; the greens like *Cymbidium* President Wilson 'Concolor' and *Cymbidium* Esmeralda; the pale yellows such as *Cymbidium* Alexanderi 'Aureum' and the whites like *Cymbidium* Alexanderi 'McBean's'. Poor things, really, compared with modern hybrids.

From the few known tetraploid cymbidiums, such as *Cymbidium* Alexanderi, *Cymbidium* Pauwelsii and *Cymbidium* Rosanna, many more were created and found. From 1960 the use of the originals dropped away to a fraction of the previous twenty years. That does not mean the originals lost anything; they are still in cultivation and it would indeed be foolish to lose sight of them.

From a tetraploid *Cymbidium Pauwelsii* came *Cymbidium* Babylon, the influence of which is strong in breeding lines. *Cymbidium* Balkis, of course, became the most used of them all, with 194 hybrids in the ten-year period 1960-70 and endless others derived from its seedlings.

While looking at influential parents, another must be included — *Cymbidium* Rio Rita 'Radiant', which is only a secondary hybrid from the natural hybrid or species *Cymbidium ruby*. *Cymbidium* Rio Rita is also supposed to be a tetraploid.

If a fraction of the work devoted to the cattleya or paphiopedilum groups had been switched to cymbidiums, it may have saved a lot of time when the whole of the British projects were discarded, disposed of, and lost in the deplorable waste of the second world war. If anything, the European collections were even more severely dealt with. The British material which went to America fired them with an appreciation of cymbidiums, almost non-existent up to that time. While the American hybridisers wasted a lot of time on things which had already been done, the results of which were obvious in the cymbidiums exported from Britain to Australia, they did bring the threads together and later produced very fine cymbidiums known all over the world. They also brought into being a market for cymbidium flowers in America.

The advent of air travel and freight made cymbidiums a useful proposition for the Australian grower in the markets of America, Europe and later Japan and other parts of Asia. The bulk of these export flowers are grown in New South Wales, and other countries in the southern hemisphere with similar climates should be most suitable for mass-production of the flowers. Other parts of Australia also produce their quota for the overseas markets.

Remembering over a long life associated with flowers, I find a parallel for cymbidiums. In the years 1918 to about 1928 my father grew gladioli, among other things, hundreds of them. Over the years he vainly tried to keep abreast of the development, even breeding some himself. I never grew gladioli, but I see them in 1979 as something where there is nowhere else to go. They are most beautiful. They started with small species, in the same way as cymbidiums, and reached an ultimate in perfection. This could be taken as the eternal cry of the old 'Is there anything yet to see?' But despite that thought, the parallel persists in my mind that, although there are certain to be new cymbidiums, just as there are new gladioli, there is perhaps a sameness there which, once reached, leaves nothing new to find. Many, perhaps will disagree, but I am afraid they will have a hard time proving their point.

Potting cymbidiums is not really difficult, but the first thing to understand is that they do not grow in 'earth' as other plants do. Over the years of looking at beginners' plants, this is the thing most of them missed. Perhaps it was the way out of a problem, but it seldom works.

Orchid growers, if they take notice of what goes on around them, find something new turning up all the time and pots, as well as materials, have changed. The day is long gone when the test of a well-potted plant was to lift it up by the leaves. As materials like Osmunda fern fibre and tan-bark became scarce, other things were found as substitutes.

As cymbidiums occur in forest areas rich in decaying material, there is good reason for this being considered the base material. Modification of this growing humus by adding drainage material, such as gravel, crushed brick, coarse sand and smaller grades of pine or fir bark, is necessary because they are to be grown in pots. Excess water should flow freely through the 'mix' and out of the drainage holes, leaving moist material to feed the roots.

Crocking the base of most plastic pots is unnecessary, but clay pots with a central drainage hole should have a few pieces of broken pot placed over the hole, after it has been enlarged to three times the diameter of the hole usually pierced in clay pots. The hole should be not less than 15 millimetres wide.

A very simple mix may be made up with one part peat-moss, one part rice hulls or peanut shells and one part gravel. It can be individually modified, some growers preferring more or less gravel, depending on their watering habits. Commercial suppliers of ready-mix potting mediums all have their own blends and although they may recommend them, they do not necessarily suit everyone. Rice hulls break down very quickly for some growers, who will prefer a more durable material like peanut shells. These also break down quickly if they are processed into too fine a grade before they are used.

Each of the materials has a number of variations. The faster decaying vegetable matter may be foliage of deciduous trees such as oak, ash, maple, plane, dry eucalypt leaves, tea-tree leaf, acacia leaves, bracken-fern or treefern frond, and many other leaves mixed with rice hulls, peanut shells or slow decay material such as fine pine bark. The best of the leaves is probably oak. Strongly acid leaves, pine needles, casuarina needles, humus and fine leaf-mould are second best and should be well weathered.

Fast decaying material should be backed up in the mix by an increase of more durable vegetable matter, such as peanut shells, pine bark, rice hulls, fir bark, and a little more drainage material, such as fine sandy gravel, even beyond the equal third parts if necessary. Leaf content should be chopped up; a simple way of doing this is to get a stack of leaves on the garage floor or on a flat concrete area and attack it with the motor mower. This does scatter it a bit and blow it about, but if a screen can be put up around the area it helps. The motor mower soon reduces it to particle size, shredded fibrous material and chopped up leaves. This leaf content should not be rotted and when measured should be pressed down into the bucket or measure used. Some growers do not use leaves, decayed or whole, as a matter of choice, the reason given being that such vegetable matter contains, or may contain, virus. There is no real basis for this view, as it is a primary natural food of all plants. Some growers go all the way and sterilise their mix.

The second material, the slower decaying part, offers a fairly wide choice. Tan bark, if it is obtainable, is still one of the best. Most of the bark used in tanneries is quite safe to use direct from the pits, but some prefer to weather it for a few months before use. It is rather slimy straight from the pits but, having used it for many years that way, I find that it has no ill effects. It is usually a mixture of fibrous material, dust and lumpy material and it should all go into the mix. Mostly it is of just the right acidity to suit cymbidiums. Several commercial grades of shredded and macerated wood chips are available and in making up a potting medium for a large number of plants it may work out a little cheaper than tan bark. Pine bark is also bagged in three or more grades and is just as good as tan bark for the purposes of backing up the less durable part of the medium. Any material used to replace the more durable vegetable component should not have quick break-down characteristics. Rice hulls are durable provided they are blended with another durable material and not blended with too high a proportion of quick-decaying foliage or vegetation. The same is true of peanut shells.

All this may be avoided by buying ready-mix from orchid nurseries. For a small number of plants it is less expensive, as by the time all the materials are collected, blended and used it could take some time and expense to get them all in your bin. Most nursery mixes are proved. There is, however, a lot to be said for blending your own and peat moss, gravel and rice hulls are usually obtainable, but it may take a bit of travelling to locate them all. Clubbing together with other smaller growers is a good way to get over the difficulty.

The most constant material in all the mixes is pine bark, once a by-product for which there seemed little use. It is at present marketed in a number of ways, from a very good substitute for peat moss to coarse chunks for garden masking, or use as potting material for vandas and orchids which have large root systems.

Sawdust mixes have been detailed many times in the last few decades and, though they have had temporary success with some growers, they are mostly individual blends and not systems in general use. They are not particularly suitable for beginners, who tend to water them too much. The preparation of most sawdust mixes ensures a fast break-down of the material, which is what most growers do not want. It has a poor enough pot life as it is. Nevertheless, it is detailed in the list.

Buzzer chips, which are another, coarser form of sawdust, may take a little longer to break down, but both sawdust and buzzer chip mixes start off the same way with an accelerated break down in the first stages.

Small shredders are available to the home gardener and tree prunings and twigs fed through these produce a very good additive to the coarser parts of the medium. Deciduous tree cuttings of many kinds can be fed into this, the best again being oak cuttings. These shredders are a very easy way to make up a potting mixture for large collections of cymbidiums and are a lot easier than shovelling the materials about on the garage floor or a convenient slab.

Whatever is made up, the quantities should be measured and noted. The mix should be turned over and over until all the components are thoroughly blended, then moistened with the hose and again turned over a few times. The heap should be flattened and spread out to a depth of about 15 centimetres. If fertilisers are used they should then be spread evenly over the surface and the heap shovelled over again several times, and left in a flat 15 centimetre-deep spread for an hour or so. It should then be felt for texture and a handful should be springy and not remain compressed or tightly bedded in the hand. It should also be moist right through without being wet. At this stage it may be bagged or used straight away. Plastic bags should be used so that the mix does not dry out again before being used.

This potting medium should be easy to work into root systems and the plants firmly potted. If the mix is springy and properly blended it is almost impossible to pot too tightly. Do not leave air pockets when using it, as these will cause the pots to dry out quickly. They will also dry out quickly if the material is not packed tightly enough.

The gravelly, sandy part of the potting medium should not be too fine or too coarse, but should be of particles from sand up to coarse 5 millimetre grains, without too much of either extreme. Scoria is ideal, black or red, but lava or basalt is not recommended because it may have a sulphur content.

Each of the one-third parts may be varied quite a lot, but whatever is added or taken away should maintain that proportion until a new system is adopted or the mix is modified to suit your growing methods. Always give a mix a fair trial before discarding it for another that some other grower recommends. The new one may not suit you at all.

Anyone with a few plants can make up a personal mix quite easily with natural materials gathered in light forest areas. Eucalypt detritus, with its mixture of leaves, twigs and small nuts, is ideal roughage; gravel or similar material is usually available and the decay portion can be made up with shredded bracken fern fronds. If the plants are grown outdoors, this is a natural growth formula for them, all that needs to be added is some form of fertiliser.

All in all, the outdoor grower has an advantage, because the materials used tend to last longer and the plants grow harder. But always try to maintain the proportions of the materials. It is not essential to incorporate manures in any of the mixes except those using sawdust or buzzer chips. These two formulas need the organic fertilisers to assist the break-down process. Added fertilisers for bark or other mixes can be selected from a wide range of organic and inorganic compounds.

Some forms of fertilisers with slow-release characteristics are not altogether suitable for cymbidiums or other orchids because they continue to release fertiliser into the potting material even when the plants are unreceptive. Cymbidiums are quite different from annual or perennial garden plants, with too much fertiliser quickly reacting against the roots contained in the restriction of a pot as against open soil. Unless a large number of plants are grown, it is best to concentrate on twice-yearly applications of fertiliser which suit the stages of growth and flowering.

Some general fertilisers like hoof and horn should be incorporated because they have a slow break-down rate. It is common to use a different fertiliser for the growing period as against the flowering period, when more phosphate is needed. Blood and bone, regarded by some growers as a 'dirty' material in orchid growing, is nevertheless a very efficient quick-release fertiliser when worked into the top of the potting medium, but it is too fast in its decay rate to use as an addition on the mixing floor in preparing a compost.

Most packets of inorganic fertilisers have the analysis printed on the packet, but on their own they are not always effective. Some also contain organic materials like hoof and horn and blood and bone. Some commercial potting mixes have fertiliser in the blend, so be careful about adding more. When buying ready-mix, if there is nothing on the packet or bag, ask the vendor what it contains.

Fowl manure should be used with a certain amount of care, as it will burn the roots if used when too fresh. While a time limit cannot be set for lapse between dropping and use, it is better to stack it for some twelve months until it rots to a soft brown 'earth'. Cow manure should be old and hard and chopped into chunks. In this form it remains as chunks and finer parts and slowly decays. In effect, it joins the primary one-third decay part of the mix with leaf mould and fine material. It can be overdone, but in the old dry state it has lost quite a lot of the quick-release fertiliser of fresh cow manure. Prepared cow manure bought from nursery suppliers is usually in powder form, sometimes sterilised, sometimes not, and is added to the decay portion. It adds to the fine portion and may need balancing with a little more gravel. Sheep manure is usually sold in this form and should be similarly treated.

Although the risk is there, there is no real basis for the prejudice of some growers who say that these fertilisers could cause virus infection of the plants. It is no more a risk than any of the other materials used.

Most people stumble over the amount of these organic fertilisers to use when making up a mix. It is better to start with a moderate amount of one part for every ten parts of the decay portion. This is where taking notes is useful. Do not trust your memory, but keep a diary of the processes and your plants. Years later you will find it useful and refreshing to look back on.

Periodically reference is made to magnesium sulphate as a cymbidium fertiliser. It has no standing as such and should be regarded merely as a link in a potting medium that was missing before its addition. It is part of the fertiliser complex.

Fertilisers are sometimes used as forcing agents. Forcing of any sort in horticulture always shows up in propagation. In cymbidium culture it may produce vigorous growth and larger flowers, but this can be dangerous and in the end result in virus infection, plant loss, or dissatisfaction of people who may later buy propagations of the plant. It should be used only when necessary.

There are several liquid nutrients on sale, some of which are mixed by dry measure, some by liquid measure. They should be used carefully until their effects are understood and always at strengths below those recommended on the containers.

Fertiliser pellets are not a suitable way to apply nutrients because they tend to localise and concentrate the plant food into too narrow a part of the potting medium. If additions are used, it is better to spread them evenly over the surface of the medium and work them into the top layer so that they slowly dissolve each time the plant is watered. If the fertiliser is placed toward the bottom of the pot it may form a concentration too strong for the plant in repotting, and by the time the roots work their way into the bottom layers it will mostly have washed out. Watering it through the mix is the best way.

Most orchid cultural literature mentions NPK ratios. Simplified, this means the proportions of nitrogen, phosphorus and potassium present in any compound. It is often expressed as 30:10:10 or some other figure, which literally means that there is three times more nitrogen than the other two available as plant food. Varying figures appear on fertiliser packets. The nitrogen is sometimes in the form of ammonium sulphate or nitrate, the potassium in the form of potash or potassium nitrate or some other compound, and the phosphorus mostly in the form of superphosphate. These three elements are the principal ones which assist plant growth and flowering, but several trace elements are also necessary for complete plant health and good flowering. Most of these elements and the trace elements are present to an extent in organic fertilisers such as fowl and animal manures. They are also present to some degree in decaying vegetation because nothing is wasted in nature, it is continually recycled.

Some idea of the amount of solid fertiliser applied as an inorganic mix, that is, a compound of chemical and sometimes animal residues like hoof and horn, needed to keep a cymbidium plant in health and prepared for flowering, is one large heaped teaspoonful of a complete fertiliser like Gro-plus or Mag-amp in October and again in March. Worked into the potting medium for a plant in a 20-25 centimetres pot, it will supply all its needs.

One last word on fertilisers, however: apply them at the right period of the year; do not mix them and hope that the plants will sort them out, and do not vary each year in the type used. One good fertiliser is all that is necessary. The plant supplier should be your guide in the initial stages, and as experience is gained, some personal sorting out and preference will soon eventuate as the plants indicate. Above all, cymbidiums growing in pots for years cannot be expected to keep flowering, or even commence flowering, if they are not fertilised.

A few of the commonly used mixes, which could be the basis of some inventiveness by beginners as well as more advanced growers, are as follows:

If tan bark is available, one part of this material, one part leaf or decay material and one part gravel is a good starting point. It may look stony, but this is not such a bad thing. The tan bark should not be too fine. The gravel portion could be replaced with scoria or a mixture of scoria and charcoal. Occasionally polyurethane beads are specified. The size of these is about small pea to finer and they can be bought freely from plastics shops or warehouses. Potting mediums containing these beads are a bit hard to handle when watering because they tend to float or splash out. They do not add anything to the mixture except drainage and are not a means of stabilising the temperature of any potting medium, although they are not subject to temperature fluctuations as much as other materials. They also tend to remain isolated in the mix which contains them.

Peat moss is another basic which is becoming scarce and dear. If it is used it usually takes the place of the decay portion of the mix and additional fertiliser is needed to compensate for this. The peat moss should be fined out so there are no lumps and again one-third of the mix will be this material. The other two parts may be pine bark and gravel in equal quantities. A variation of this is to halve the peat moss and make up the quantity with peanut shells or rice hulls or a mixture of both. Again charcoal or plastic beads may be used in the drainage material in proportions to suit the grower.

If organic fertilisers are used with either of these two mixes they should comprise part of the decay portion. The grade of pine bark used should be small, but not too fine. Another pine bark material has been introduced recently to take the place of peat moss. As yet it is unproved, but should be quite serviceable. It would be better used in a tan bark mix than in a pine bark mix, but could be used either way if it proves successful.

Most of these basics are easily obtained and the only two which might tend to bind together and pack too firmly are the two forms of pine bark — the ordinary coarse 5-10 millimetres aggregate and the fine peat moss replacement material. Any of these mixes may have the decay portion replaced by a mixture of leaf choppings, or have these included as a replacement for part of the peanut shells and rice hulls.

Potting mixtures which should be treated with a degree of care are those made from sawdust or fine wood shavings. A great deal of this material is from processing Australian hardwood, which breaks down very quickly.

The first of these is made up of gravelly sand, sawdust and fowl manure — four parts each of sand and sawdust, and one and a half of fowl manure, preferably fresh but not decayed. These materials are thoroughly mixed and dampened and turned over every four or five days. As a considerable amount of heat is generated, the heap should be covered. At the end of four weeks, when the heat has entirely gone out of the mix, it may be used. The quantities may be varied considerably to suit different growers. This is a quick-rotting mix, although one from which excellent results have been shown. It is capable also of modification in the fertilisers used. Hoof and horn as well as blood and bone or plain bone meal may also be added. It can also be used as a blend to replace the quick-rotting portion of the mediums already given. The main feature of this mix is the maturing period, which is essential in the preparation.

The second mix contains buzzer chips instead of sawdust in a blend containing tan bark, fir bark or pine bark. Fowl manure is added in the same amount and the blend takes the same time to mature. Although the buzzer chips should be the major part, it can be left to the individual to make a mix which suits. The proportion of sand or gravel should be kept fairly high, however, as the buzzer chips soon turn to decayed wood.

Generally speaking, both these mixtures, although simple for a grower with only a few plants or a small collection, are not the advisable potting material. They are quite safe when used with understanding, but for anything other than controlled glass-house conditions, they will quickly waterlog, particularly in open or shade-house cultivation. When and how much to water is the key and a mistake is almost certainly drastic.

There are hundreds of variations of the quoted potting mediums and it is up to each grower to sort out what suits his or her particular environment. The outdoor grower with a few plants is much more easily satisfied than one with a large collection and aspirations to prize-winning standards. Perhaps the most important thing to remember is that cymbidium roots are replaced almost annually and if the developing system is damaged there is little chance of putting it right in that year. The wood, sawdust or buzzer chip mediums are less forgiving than those with a more open texture and no pre-rotted stage in preparation.

Whatever potting medium is used or designed, it must fulfil several roles. It must support the plant; there should be no tendency for the pot to become waterlogged when watered, even if initially the material might be quite wet; drain well; promote root growth, and to this end should be tested with a small propagation or plant with growing root tips before it is adopted as a general mix. Root growth should be examined by pushing out small plants on to the palm of the hand at intervals to see what is going on.

Fertilisers should be understood before they are used, or misused, and the medium should be capable of a pot life of at least three years. Preferably the surface of the material should compact and not wash out when lightly watered with a hose. If this is caused by some of the components, a topping of 2 centimetres of bark should be used over the lighter material.

No cymbidium plant should be allowed to reach this stage. It is overgrown, full of useless pseudo-bulbs, most of which will soon become leafless back-bulbs. At times growers are prone to leave un-flowered plants intact in the hope that they will flower in the next season. This is a mistake, as there is so little useful mix in the pot that it cannot flower without supplements. Such plants frequently are forced into flower if carefully dis-membered about the beginning to the end of January, but this is far from an infallible way to make obdurate plants flower.

The correct stage at which a plant should be repotted. Several of the back-bulbs are quite leafless while all the others are in good leaf, there are three new partly developed pseudo-bulbs and if the plant is handled carefully there should be no setback to flowering. While it may be hard to gauge the sized pot the plant here occupies, it is a large growing hybrid in a 25 centimetre (10 inch) pot, which it has occupied for two years. Most potting mixes have broken down to unacceptable levels after three years and should be handled as a matter of routine.

After drying out for a week or a little longer the plant is easily removed from the pot by laying it on its side and pushing up from the bottom or grasping the old bulbs firmly and pulling. It has a nice white clean root system and from the porous look of the mix this conditin should be expected even in the centre of the root mass. The new shoots on the roots show that the correct time has been selected to carry out the break-up. This should be a matter of course, as the plant is too large and has so many leafless back-bulbs that no other plan should be thought of.

61

After being lightly beaten on the ground the dry mix shakes out of the roots very well and the whole root system is obviously falling apart. When picking up a plant by the leaves to beat it on the ground only the older leaves should be grasped and sufficient care taken to see that the new leads or the root tips on new shoots, if there are any, are not damaged, as these are quite tender. When sufficient material has been loosened from the root ball some trial grips should be taken on the plant to see where it will break most economically.

After initially loosening up the root ball, if the plant has been dried out properly before starting the process, fingers may be used to poke out most of the old potting material and loosen up the root ball. Quite a lot of untangling may be done at this stage, and this always benefits the root system and subsequent plant recovery.

Although the plant has not divided evenly into two portions, it has broken into two parts at a natural break which leaves both with good prospects of flowering despite the potting process. The root system is also parting without too much trouble and little breakage. By gently shaking and pulling the two propagations apart, the job is soon completed. A clearer picture of the two pieces is also apparent, showing that the interior of the root mass is just as healthy as the outside.

The smaller of the two propagations, stripped of the two back-bulbs and all useless roots, comprises an old bulb hidden behind the new shoot and a mature bulb to which is attached the stump of a flower spike from a few months before. Where the major break occurred and on the raw breaks left by the removal of the back-bulbs some anti-fungus powder and lime was rubbed in. This plant was handled in January and the bulb which has the old spike stump subsequently showed another spike from the other side of the bulb in March, as well as pushing up the new lead for the following season's flowering.

The two propagations correctly potted, the larger one returned to the pot from which the whole plant was removed. In each instance the root system was comfortably fitted and that was all. Although all the back-bulbs were removed from the smaller of the two portions, they were left attached to the larger piece, but with all their roots removed so they could be taken out without problems at any time later. The height of the plants in the pots is correct, with the bases of the bulbs just below the rim.

A pot should be like a hat — it should fit without being too tight or too loose. In this example the plant may seem a little large for the pot containing it, but after the mix has been trickled down into the gap in the foreground of the photo until it is fairly firm, the plant should be forced back on to this and that part of the pot farthest from the camera left for the plant to fill after it has been also filled and firmed with the potting mix. Make sure that the whole root system is filled by poking it in with fingers until no more can be pushed into the roots.

The slim, wedge-like taper of the growth on the right of the new bulb is quite different from the blunt flower spikes emerging from the same bulb in this photograph. While some cymbidiums flower more readily and freely than others, this plant was portion of a large break-up about the beginning of December and the flower spikes were visible at the end of January. Where they can be purchased, regardless of the type of flowers produced, these easy flowering plants are the ones for outdoor growing.

The tough fibrous core of a cymbidium back-bulb is similar to the bony base of vertebrates — it outlasts the rest of the construction by a long period. Even the wasting brown rot infections have little effect on these tough fibres.

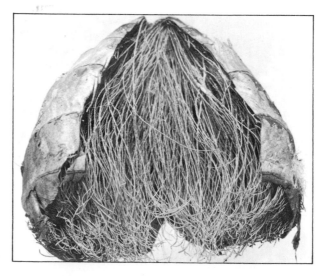

64

# Watering

Potting materials, however good, can be quickly ruined by poor watering methods. Some are designed to be kept moist, but if the root system is killed off even these turn sour and useless.

Little thought is given to the quality of water, but it should be considered. Most reticulated supplies should be suspect and under test may show up deficiencies. Some may even have unwanted additives like chlorine. Others, including most bore supplies, are too alkaline and totally unsuitable. If cymbidiums do not thrive, the water should be tested. The local chemist or sections of the agricultural departments can usually say where this can be done. The water should be slightly acid or neutral, never so much as a suggestion alkaline. A bad test report means that rainwater should be used, because it is too expensive to change mains or bore supplies.

When to water cymbidiums or, for that matter, any orchids, is a constant question. It is easily answered but poorly understood. The answer is to water when the plants need it. Each grower is faced with a different set of growing conditions, dictated by situation, a protected or unprotected environment, the amount of shade the plants have, the potting materials used, and so many other things, that the simple answer is the only one possible. Watering must be a personal, weather-dictated operation to be solved sensibly.

Cymbidiums do not soak up great quantities of water like other plants and trees. They have an inbuilt system for protecting themselves and people who habitually cut off all the old bulbs defeat this protection system.

Reference to habitat conditions is partly a lead but, as we grow cymbidiums like terrestrial plants at about sea level mostly, instead of duplicating their epiphytic habits in semi-tropical and tropical highlands, some compromise is necessary. It is possible to overwater in the growing period of October to March just as easily as in the cooler and flowering or semi-dormant part of their cycle from March to October. The possibility of overwatering is intensified by the natural shift into readily obtainable and more durable plastic pots.

If cymbidiums are grown in open conditions where a summer rainfall pattern is usual they may go for a considerable period without hand watering. If the rainfall pattern is winter and the plants are grown outdoors, there is no real need to worry about the amount they receive provided the drainage system is good. But if the rainfall pattern of summer is sparse and the weather hot the plants may need watering every second day, with considerable moisture applied to the surroundings during the day. The old method of 'looking at' and 'poking at' is probably the best approach. Poke about in the surface of the potting material and if it is damp then the plant needs no more water for a day or so. It certainly will not fade away or die.

When the plants are watered, make sure that the water is applied over the entire surface and that it flows out freely from the bottom. The process can be repeated again without any reason for alarm. Thoroughly water each plant and, if the weather is hot and dry, be prepared to water them again the following day. Never stand the plants in saucers or dishes of water. If anything is done in that direction it should be to stand the pot on a moist surface of whatever type.

Cymbidium plants aerate the growing medium by their root action. As soon as the roots are halted or damaged, the potting medium becomes dead and soggy, and soon turns sour. Further root damage then follows. Overwatering is probably the only cause of root damage provided, of course, that the water is not alkaline or unsuitable in some other way.

Plants which are bought or otherwise acquired already potted and growing are frequently mishandled by beginners, who sometimes imagine that because they are large plants they will need plenty of water. This they proceed to give them. In a matter of two weeks such damage has been done to the root system that it is reparable only by taking the plant apart and starting it, or pieces of it, away again. So begins the disillusionment of many would-be or prospective orchid growers.

Unfortunately, there are no indicators which appear quickly to tell the plant killer what he or she is doing. Later the leaf tips will yellow and then turn brown and some of the leaves will do the same. By that time the major portion of the roots are quite dead, the plant does not flower in its turn, and slowly fades away into back-bulbs. Occasionally the reverse happens if the season for it coincides with the mishandling. The plant will send up spikes of flower which are the last that will appear for a long time.

Sometimes the habit of the plant in casting leaves worries the outdoor fancier or beginner. It is a natural habit for cymbidiums to cast some leaves on the older bulbs in the growing season, even to the extent of casting them all off the really old bulbs. However, if these leaves are cast in abnormal numbers, the cause can usually be put down to overwatering. If the shade is insufficient they will turn yellow but are not always cast.

In average glass-house conditions in summer, using plastic pots with free drainage medium, 60 or 80 per cent shade, and free ventilation, a thorough watering every three or four days should be sufficient to keep the plants in good condition. They may not need this frequency, or they may need more. The poke and look system should be applied here, too. In average open conditions with a summer rainfall pattern there is no necessity to water at all until some three or four days have elapsed since the last rain fell, provided it was soaking rain and not just a shower.

Much of the watering process — perhaps it should be called moisture maintenance — of cymbidiums should be atmospheric. This is easier to handle in a glass-house than outdoors, especially in hot, dry areas. In these conditions a night watering or misting system should be operated to take the place of normal condensation or dew formation in better climates, so that even if plants cannot be given all the necessary features of an ideal climate they can perhaps be tricked by some resemblance to those conditions. This can be helped by the nature of the floor or even the ground on which outdoor plants are grown. If a solid floor is chosen for a glass-house it should be of cinder bricks or other absorptive material, as ordinary concrete dries out too fast. The plants should be grown as near the moist floor as possible, in keeping with the type of enclosure, anything from direct contact to about 30 centimetres. In such a position the humidity is much better and the plants remain moist for longer periods provided the floor is kept damp.

Overhead spraying is favored by some growers. This may be done several times a day, but always see that the foliage is as dry as possible before nightfall, particularly in colder climates. It is almost impossible to overdo the humidity in relatively even temperatures of 15-20 degrees Celsius (approximately 60-70 degrees Fahrenheit), but when the temperature soars to the high 30 degrees Celsius (80-90 degrees Fahrenheit) and beyond, scalding could occur.

Overhead spraying or damping down is largely a matter of preference and the same effect can be had with adequate shade, good ventilation and a wet to damp floor.

A light intensity in bright sunny weather of higher than that imparted with 60 per cent shade-cloth should be regarded as chancy, and could mean more frequent watering and damping down. Light intensity moderated by shade-cloth is most variable and we can only take the manufacturer's word for it that any percentage is so. With painted roofs the guesswork is intensified, because the amount of paint put on will also alter a reading. A painted roof could be anything from 30 per cent shade to 80 per cent, the watering period in both instances dicatated again more by poke and feel and the floor dampened down as needed during each day.

A rough-and-ready measure for the amount of shade needed to cultivate cymbidiums is to put a sheet of white paper on the bench, or on top of the plants, and a hand held 30 centimetres (12 inches) above that paper should not cast a shadow.

As shade and watering go hand in hand, they should be the guide, one for the other. If the plants dry out too fast the shade is insufficient. If they stay wet too long, it is too dense and the foliage will soon turn dark green. The airflow adds to these factors, but for cymbidiums it should be good.

Watering indicators, which show how much moisture is held in the potting material, are used by some growers and while they could be handy where consistent pot sizes occur, they could be misleading unless used on every pot in the collection. Mostly these indicators are prod type, with a dial reading indicating just how moist the medium is. A hygrometer, which measures atmospheric moisture or humidity, can also be used in a glass-house. These are also usually dial-indicator instruments, but are more useful in glass-houses for epiphytic orchids like cattleyas and dendrobiums than cymbidiums. A good indicator is a potful of the medium being used. It is pressed into a pot, the same as if it held a plant. This potful of material should be soaked in the same way as the rest of the collection, pressed out and examined if there is any doubt about watering. It should be an average sized pot in the group.

A good rule to follow is that if there is any doubt, do not water the plants. Water the floor and the benches thoroughly, and perhaps give the foliage a misting over so there is no further loss of moisture to the atmosphere.

Probably some growers wonder what happens if the plant is allowed to dry out and remain too dry for a period. In this case the roots seal themselves off so that they do

When watering cymbidiums it is as well to keep the flowers dry. This one is creamy yellow and could easily mark.

not surrender moisture any more than necessary to the potting material. They may take anything up to three weeks or more to renew activity. In this period overwatering is just as dangerous as in the instance of too-wet plants.

The potting medium will probably shrink if allowed to become over-dry and it takes time to swell out again. This is the basis of the recommendation that the ideal condition is for a stable, moist condition of the material, maintained by a consistent watering pattern which allows flooding and the draining of excess water from both the pot and the potting material. In some ways a collection of growing cymbidiums in all sized pots and all sized plants is a constant hazard unless they are sorted out. It may not suit the appearance of the collection or, at times, certain plants, but it does avoid the trap which may lead to overwatering of some plants and too little for others.

Single plants are always much harder to judge for moisture than a collection, so there is only one way to try them — poke and pry. If such a plant is grown under a tree it can be left very much to nature to supply its needs. Only in dry periods is there any need to water it, and usually it can be looked after at the same time as the garden is watered.

Open-structure or shade-house growers have no worries about ventilation, but in designing or erecting a kit glass-house, it should be one of the major considerations. Roof ventilation as well as wall ventilation should be allowed for most orchids.

In their natural habitats cymbidiums grow in mixed groups of terrestrial, lithophytic and epiphytic plants where airflow is constant and the whole ecosystem has an atmosphere or 'smell'. The smell is one of the things which must be built into the glasshouse. Cymbidiums are lower strata plants, sometimes almost wholly terrestrial like *Cymbidium insigne*. Even at this lowest level in the system there is air movement and it may have to be induced in the growing area, as suggested previously.

*A few points about watering are worth noting:*

Whatever water is used should preferably be tested. It should be neutral or slightly acid, never alkaline. If the last is all that is available, some effort should be made to alter it if necessary if cymbidiums are to be grown to flowering stage.

Cymbidiums should not be allowed to dry right out before being again watered. In outdoor or open-air growing, some thought should be given to the relative humidity of the immediate surroundings in a hot, dry climate. Watering the surroundings frequently will keep the humidity a little higher.

Some attempt should be made to enclose an area if trees or other natural cover are not obtainable to give speckled light. See the illustrations for what can be done in this regard.

In hot climates, night watering should be tried as a method of inducing the plants to flower. The basis is for cooling the pot rather than humidifying. Misting over the leaves might also have a beneficial effect.

Root loss and plant shrivelling is caused more by overwatering than anything else.

Plastic and clay pots should not be used together in a collection.

Overhead watering or misting should be avoided in cold weather, and if carried out in the dormant or cooler part of the year it should be done in the morning, so that the foliage is dry by nightfall.

Do not close the ventilators of a damp or wet glass-house in winter. The better the airflow, small as it may be, the less likelihood of plant damage.

There is little that can be done to protect outdoor plants from cold and wet winter weather. Although this could mean collapse of a project designed along these lines, it is worth a try and a lot of people underestimate their climate and its possibilities.

Watering is closely allied to the type of potting medium in use. Always try to have only one mix, even if it means repotting plants out of season.

It is fairly easy to tell by the weight of a pot whether it is dry or not — make a habit of picking up the various sizes and feeling their weight. A little experience and no diffidence soon gives a grower the 'feel' of a dry or wet pot.

Propagation should be understood to mean correct growing just as much as the cutting and multiplying processes. No poorly propagated cymbidium thrives, and as much thought should be given to that one problem plant as the large collection.

Cymbidium plants can be bought in all stages, from seedlings and what are called 'meristems', up to large, overgrown masses of bulbs. The last-mentioned are, together with leafless back-bulbs, the worst way to begin growing orchids. For a number of reasons, when cymbidiums develop naturally into large specimens, growers become afraid of them. 'What do I do with them?', they ask. Like some other stages in orchid growing, this one persists even with experienced growers and plant handlers. Everyone would prefer a simpler propagating specimen. Frequently the owners of such plants sell them rather than take them apart, particularly if they are survivors from a past and long-gone generation. The natural answer, of course, is to keep all the plants in a condition which is easily handled.

Having acquired such a plant, the hobbyist is best advised to look at the pictures and carry out dividing and repotting as though it had been done many times before. Normally, any plant will indicate, by the position of the non-leafed bulbs and the green bulbs, the place where it will divide itself. Preferably attack it in the area of the leafless bulbs if it is intended to cut it up with a large knife. Do not try to make too many plants from the large one and unless the back-bulbs — the term used to denote the leafless parts of the plant — are fairly recent, it may not be a good idea to try cultivating plants from them.

If you are a beginner and someone offers you a back-bulb as a starter in the hobby, in a moderate climate such as that of the southern parts of Australia, it is indeed a poor start. If it is your choice, buy a larger plant, preferably of three or four leafed bulbs and several back-bulbs, even up to the frightening large size. It does not matter how cheap or poor looking the flowers from these plants are, they are the ones on which you can learn all the valuable lessons.

One of the first things is to understand the nature of the plant itself. Like all orchids, cymbidiums prefer to grow into large plants without interruption. They also flower best this way and, although it is unsuitable for glass-house growing, a balance must be struck between what the plants like and what the grower wants from them.

As described earlier, cymbidiums are not unlike iris plants; each forms a rhizome with growths appearing from it at intervals. In the case of cymbidiums, these growths fatten out into what are known as pseudo-bulbs or bulbs. The function of these bulbs is to produce flower spikes and also produce growths from the lower part for another extension of the rhizome.

A further function of these bulbs is to act as a reservoir of sap and moisture to counter adverse weather cycles and dry periods, which occur in countries where they originate. They perform this function for us in periods of poor cultivation. Even when leaves are cast from the bulbs in their final cycle of life, they still act in this way Unlike bulbs such as onions, which are layered or laminated in construction and are quite squashy, cymbidium bulbs are very fibrous and tough, even if most of their bulb is made up of moisture. They are also very durable, withstanding droughts, fires and floods, and still able to produce shoots from eyes at their bases.

On growing plants, these back-bulbs are good indicators of the real state of the plant. When they turn dark in their aged state they should also be watched for signs of softness, which indicates disease. If soft when squeezed they should be removed and the base disinfected with anti-fungus powder and lime and allowed to dry out, so that the rot does not progress downward into the rhizome. Any suspicion of rot can be satisfied by cutting about 5 millimetres off the top. If it is still green and healthy looking, rub anti-fungus powder and lime into this surface also.

There is a relationship between the area and health of the roots and that of the leaves of cymbidiums, therefore the leaves should be cared for and held on the plant as long as possible. Although they also are tough, they may be easily broken, bent, or damaged and burnt by the sun or disease.

Most cymbidiums grown are hybrids, some removed more than ten times from their species progenitors. To a degree, they are the product of their environment and will not grow or have the best flowers in anything but the best of conditions.

When and how a plant should be propagated and grown because it has outlived its container is shown in the illustrations, but a further description is possibly a good idea.

The best plants and flowers usually appear on propagations which have been grown on from small pieces by a series of steps. The first of these is to select the best portion of a plant and pot it into as small a pot as will take the root system. The time taken to propagate a plant to maturity is relative to the size and health of the piece and the care in its handling.

Beginning at the lowest end of the scale, a back-bulb, that is, a bulb which has lost all its leaves and roots, is the worst possible start from which to grow a flowering plant. On average, it would take some three or four years to grow a reasonably sized plant and not necessarily the best which the clone may be capable of growing. It may flower after this time lapse, or it may not. Such a bulb and its resultant growth period is illustrated.

The back-bulb is followed in the sequence by a single green bulb, which is a bulb with leaves and roots. These roots should be serviceable and the bulb may be from the leading part of the plant or not. This type of propagation is also poor because it is unnatural for cymbidiums to be severed into single units; they need back-up. This type of poor propagation often results in diseased plants, but is frequently used.

The next stage in propagations would be a green leafed bulb backed up by a back-bulb, and this is quite a good start. The leafed bulb, provided it has some good roots attached, will soon call on the back-bulb to surrender its substance if necessary, to tide it over until it produces a shoot and some more roots. The real value of this back-bulb is that it is able to absorb moisture directly without roots if the propagation is grown in a good 'live' environment.

The next best propagation, of course, is two green bulbs, as they are known, both having all their root systems intact. It soon moves into growth if taken at the right season.

There are two ultimate propagations combining all the desirable characteristics for good growth. One is a green bulb and what is known as a 'lead', a half-formed new bulb; the other is a section of a plant containing leafed green bulbs, one or two back-bulbs and one or more new leads. Both of these propagations quickly commence to grow.

All these propagations have relative prices, the ultimate price depending on the scarcity, beauty or demands made on the owner of the clone.

A buyer should see that any of these propagations, except the back-bulb, have some live roots, not broken at the point of emergence from the rhizome or along their length. Broken roots are no good, despite what some vendors may say, particularly if the propagation is taken away from the source and grown in another environment by a different grower. All these propagations should be potted in containers which just take the root system in comfort.

All plants which show they must be divided into pieces should be dried out for a few days so that the potting material will mostly fall away from the roots. The root system will also toughen up if it is allowed to dry out. What comes out of most compacted pots of cymbidium plants appears as a most impenetrable mass, with the obvious inclination imparted to the would-be propagator to push it back into the pot and leave it for someone else.

The first stage is to gently dump the plant on the ground on its side to shake it up a little, then to prise away the outer roots as carefully as possible. It is unfortunate that most of these roots are the newer ones, but once loosened it is best to work into the centre of the root ball.

Naturally, there is going to be root damage. It is unavoidable and most of that which is freed will be broken and useless. However, be as careful as possible. When the root ball has been loosened and as much as possible of the potting medium shaken out, the plant should be grasped firmly by the pseudo-bulbs with little or no leaf and twisted apart. It will usually break at a natural division. The general idea is to break the plant into two parts, whether they are equal or not.

Once a break has developed, the whole plant should again be lightly flailed on the ground while pulling the two sections apart. It should be shaken and pulled until the sections release their respective root systems. A decision on whether to further divide may be made at this point along the lines of the propagations described. If the plant can be divided into several pieces, keep them within the best of those limits. If it is intended to keep the divisions for the collection, make them as large as possible so that there is probable continuity of flowering.

The root system will by now be rather limp and more easily dealt with. It should be shortened considerably and carefully until it will fit into the pot intended without the roots doubling over and breaking further. If the root system is a little longer than the pot depth it can possibly be 'screwed' down into the pot by rotating the plant in one direction and the pot in the other. Poor roots should be pruned from the base of the pseudo-bulbs rather than torn away and how much of it is still good depends on the harshness of the whole process. Some of this harshness can be taken out of the job by careful disentanglement with two pointed sticks, similar to butchers' wooden skewers. With these, although the job will take longer, the roots may be picked out individually and the whole lot finally combed out like tangled hair. I must confess that I do not have this sort of patience.

Occasionally the whole of the root system must be cut away, but always halt short of that if possible. On repotting, little of the remaining roots will have any permanence and simply tide the plant over until it can make new roots from the rhizome or new leads. It is also possible for the rhizome on the older part of the plant to produce new roots.

Pot size is sometimes a matter of locality rather than hard-and-fast rules. In New South Wales, for instance, a larger pot can be used for plant divisions than in Victoria or Tasmania. In any area where fast plant growth is possible a larger pot may be used than in colder climates where root growth is slower.

Whatever pot is selected, the pseudo-bulbs should have the base level with or just below the rim of the pot. Any higher level leaves the roots exposed and unprotected by the potting medium.

Each propagation resulting from the break-up should have a pot adequate for its size, with such things as single bulbs and back-bulbs in so small a pot that it seems out of balance. There are nearly always a few casualties, such as single bulbs and back-bulbs, in break-ups, and they develop a root system faster in small pots. It is also sometimes an advantage to have the potting medium slightly less 'boney'.

The various divisions will probably go into different sized pots and the period between their waterings will be different. When watering the small dry pots do not be tempted to water the larger ones at the same time. Go back to the poke and pry system to find out when they need it.

The root recovery rate varies with the climate and would be faster in some areas than others. It is usually a matter of three or four weeks and the plants should be kept in denser shade than the rest of the undisturbed plants, in a moist, humid atmosphere.

There is sure to be some leaf loss and a little shrivelling of the bulbs. If they shrivel to a marked degree, it usually indicates a complete failure of the root system. The plant should then be taken out of the pot, all the dead root removed and the base of the bulbs wrapped in a ball of sphagnum moss in a pot which just accommodates it. It should be staged in a cool, shady spot. If it has good forward growth new roots should again emerge in a couple of weeks, but the plant should be left in the moss ball until they are 70-80 millimetres (3-4 inches) long, when the plant may again be potted in the growing medium. Recovery may be slow and the plant may not really fatten out again until March-April, when the usual maturing process occurs. It may not flower after this setback.

Always start off in a small pot and do not be in too much of a hurry to move plants into larger pots. This is the route to good, healthy cymbidium plants which will produce the best flowers.

Some cymbidiums, particularly green-flowered varieties, do not always take kindly to repotting or break-up. They should never be allowed to overgrow into plants hard to handle. This shrivelling factor may be put down against the influence of the species *Cymbidium grandiflorum,* which is notorious for its shrivelling and root loss on handling. It also may happen with other cymbidiums getting into and past the tenth generation. The general run of cymbidiums, however, should not lose much leaf or root in careful repotting. Many hybrids have a somewhat shorter, thicker root system than the original species, and these stand the repotting process much better. They also produce their best flowers when frequently handled and are easy to pot.

The twice-through system has something to recommend it. Repotting and division is started about the beginning of October. It always helps if the glass-house for these plants is kept at about 14-15 degrees Celsius (about 60-65 degrees Fahrenheit), as the root system does better with this little bit of warmth in cooler climates. These plants can be assisted by a hot-bed if it is available, but the roots will be away within three to four weeks. They are left until the end of January and then carefully and completely repotted. There is no halt in the plant process toward flowering. In completely new mix they get away to a flying start for the autumn and winter.

This system also allows modification of the fertiliser program, as in the first repot it can be left out entirely, and put into the second one with the root systems ready to take full advantage of it. Another advantage is that it affords another chance to remove all unthrifty roots and adds a year or more to the durability of the mix. The old mix need not be completely discarded, but should be completely free from roots and rubbish, and bagged and recycled as an addition to the following year's mix.

Usually it is inadvisable to re-use old potting material. It serves as a good humus addition to the garden, the charcoal, gravel and other durable portions serving to open up heavy soils.

It is unreal to expect repotted plants to flower following repotting, but it is not unusual. The real answer lies in the plants themselves; in some instances because they flower readily, at other times they can be encouraged by careful procedures and good environments. Some cymbidiums do not flower until they have quite filled the pot with roots, in which condition they produce all their flowers in one go. It could be an inherent characteristic of *Cymbidium insigne,* because some clones grown in Australia in years past refused to flower until they were large plants. Strange as it may seem, there are even some cymbidiums which do not flower at all. I have known of clones which were grown for very many years until in desperation the owner, with as many as twenty plants — and large ones at that — cut them all up and had a bargain sale. A really bad bargain for whoever bought them. Some cymbidiums may be repotted every second season with no ill effects at all, while others may go that long before they flower again.

If it is decided to propagate a plant, it should be examined and a decision made as to the number of pieces it will make. In that growing season it should be divided between the bulbs determined as the propagations with a sharp, thin-bladed knife, sterilising the blade between each cut. The plant is then left intact until time for handling, and by that time it will have formed new growths probably with short new roots.

There is a difference between repotting and potting on. Some growers advocate complete repotting all the time, which may be a good plan with certain types of plants but not others.

In the pot-on the plant is put into a pot 50 millimetres (2 inches) or a littler larger than the one it is occupying, if the root system and the potting material are sound. The leading part of the plant should be given the benefit of the extra space and new potting material packed into the space. Two things should be watched; the potting material should be the same as that in the original pot, and there should be no air gaps left in the new material or between the old root ball and the sides of the pot where it touches.

Mostly with the granular mixes used there is no problem with the introduction of the new material and its blending into the old. The plant should also be positioned with the base of the pseudo-bulbs just below the rim of the new pot. Plants potted on should not be dried out before handling, as this would cause a lot of the granular mix to fall away. The moisture will tend to bind it together a little.

The ideal stage for potting on is when new roots are visible on the outside of the mix when the plant is pushed out. If there is a thick and complex root system on the outside and little mix visible, it would be better to completely repot the plant after untangling, trimming and rearranging the root system. This thick root mass seldom takes into a new layer of material in a pot-on and lasts only a year at best, usually finishing up with a half-decayed root system on the outside and a totally decayed system in the middle.

Potting on should not be habitual with small seedlings and meristem propagations. It is always best to renew the potting material for these small plants each time, after shaking off the old and examining and trimming the root system. The root system on these small plantlets is usually sparse, so a bit of care should be used in handling them.

Among the undesirable root conditions noticed on repotting are two in particular: the blackening of the roots, which can be caused by virus, incorrect acidity of the potting material, or water, or too much fertiliser; the other is brown and obviously rotten root predominating over good root, which can be caused by poor drainage or poor watering techniques. Slow-release fertilisers, or any fertilisers whatever, are best left out of the mix used for these plants until the systems are rectified and clean. These plants should be watched in watering, and pushed out of the pots periodically to see how they are progressing. If healthy root is visible, slow-release fertiliser should be worked into the top of the potting material. Poor root action is often caused by low temperatures in the dormant period in conjunction with too much water. Over these cold periods, if no heating system is available, the plants should be kept a little dryer than usual in a glass-house. Outdoor growers do not seem to have the same problems.

Potting tools do not amount to a great number. They should include a sharp, thin-bladed knife, a good pair of light secateurs and two or three sharpened sticks for picking apart root systems. All these tools should be sterilised before use, even after cutting one portion of a plant and moving to another. Flame sterilisation should not be used with either the knife or the secateurs, as this interferes with the temper of the blades. A good antiseptic should be bought which is effective against virus.

Although the most probable point of entry for virus is through the roots, leaves should not be handled, particularly rubbed between the fingers while handling the plants or walking through them. Other people should be told about this if they tend to do it.

Slaked lime should be rubbed into any cut surfaces of the rhizome on plants which are well regarded. Some growers also mix a fungicide with the lime. This prevents the entry of spores to the base of bulbs and the rhizome which could cause brown rot. The air is full of such spores.

If clay pots are used the old practice of covering the enlarged drainage hole should be followed, so that the potting material will not bed down into the base of the pot in an impervious mass. In plastic pots with bottom holes only, a drainage plate should be put in first before the potting material. If the pots are slotted around the sides at the base, a handful of coarse material first, then the mix, is a good idea. There is no need to crock these pots, but see that the plants drain after they are watered.

73

The back-bulb, shrivelled and leafless, the poorest of propagations to buy, but at times the one easiest afforded. While a back-bulb takes time to grow, it should produce a shoot very soon after being severed from the plant and put in a pot with a little moss or growing mix and kept damp. If no shoot is forthcoming a buyer would be within his rights in asking for a replacement. These bulbs produce shoots at times from the eyes higher up, but these are very weak and take longer to grow.

Next to the back-bulb comes almost a back-bulb with a shoot or new growth. It is a much better start because it has good working roots and when potted up will soon progress and fatten out the growth. Like any other leafed propagation, it should be critically inspected and if leaf markings are present which could indicate some sort of disease this should be pointed out to the seller. Most commercial propagators quite willingly replace unsatisfactory or diseased propagations, many, however, stipulating their guarantee period.

One of the most satisfactory propagations is a small green leafed bulb backed up with a back-bulb and showing a new lead. This soon makes up into a flowering plant. Although it is impossible to say how long it takes a propagation to get to flowering stage, an average would be about three years from a back-bulb, about two years from a small bulb with a lead, and about one year for a propagation like this one. It is well to remember, however, that to buy plants without knowing what they are is always a risk.

Each cymbidium propagation has a pot size relative to its root system or the size of the plant. In the case of a back-bulb there is little if any root and the bulb should be set into a pot taking this into account. Naturally it will not need any water, but the potting material should be kept damp, as the old bulb is able to absorb moisture. The propagation should stay in this sized pot until it has at least made up its first bulb, which may take two years or more. All the old leaf husks should be cleaned off before it is potted.

75

# Meristem
# Propagation

The ultimate phase in propagation came with the introduction of multiplication of orchid clones by shoot meristem culture. Much literature has been poured out on this.

Using the technique, it is possible to raise thousands of small duplicates of any cymbidium clone. This brings the best cymbidiums to growers very quickly, whereas at one time it took many years before saturation of demand for clones was reached. Some of the finest cymbidiums are poor propagators, but by this process they can be produced rapidly and soon may be bought in all stages, from tiny plantlets to larger propagations. They are also sometimes priced in a more reasonable bracket than when dependent on normal propagation.

The raising technique is very similar to that used in raising orchid seedlings. They are not, however, totally acceptable and have produced some problem plants. Most of these plantlets may be bought with confidence and are commonly called 'meristems'. The techniques for this process and also for seed raising are covered in many other books and are no part of this one. It extends to many other orchids than cymbidiums and originated in experiments with other plants.

The meristem process revitalised cymbidium cultivation at a time when most growers wanted, and almost needed, the better types to stock their glass-houses and growing areas. It is also part of the answers to the questions of continuity of cymbidium cultivation. In the past, large numbers of seedlings were raised and sold, but now that demand is shared with meristem production. The wise grower will have a little both ways, as there is always the delightful prospect of flowering top-grade seedling cymbidiums regardless of the odds against them. The odds are a little more realistic than they were in the early days of hybridising, or even in the middle stages, because the color range and quality is outstanding in the parents used.

Adoption of the process in Australia is fairly recent, and this abridged survey of the method is perhaps one of the few lucid accounts condensed into an understandable form for anyone who has a smattering of knowledge about horticulture. It is from a publication issued by the University of Nottingham department of horticulture, compiled by Margaret E. Marston and Pisit Voraurai:

The breeding of orchids is often a slow and costly undertaking. At least two years and as many as seven may elapse before a seedling flowers. Even then, although hundreds of seeds may be obtained from a particular cross, only a few of the progeny may be worth bulking up into a clone.

Until a few years ago multiplication has been by division or by the removal of pseudo-bulbs, which inevitably has resulted in only a few additional plants each year and consequently promising new hybrids have been sold for enormous sums of money. In fact, they have been used mainly as 'stud' plants for further hybridising. However, about 10 years ago (1957) when Professor Georges Morel cultured shoot meristems of cymbidiums under sterile conditions in vitro he found that within a few months hundreds of plantlets could be obtained from one meristem (Morel, 1960). This revolutionary discovery created intense interest amongst orchid growers and has already had considerable impact on various aspects of the orchid industry, since it is now possible to buy large numbers of young plantlets of a named variety of known performance at a relatively low cost. It is thought that this new method, known as 'meristem culture of orchids', may not only affect orchid growers throughout the world, but may also have far-reaching repercussions on other branches of horticulture.

In the last 30 years growers of many horticultural crops have had to face the problems of orchid diseases, which often cause deterioration in productivity and quality and in some cases heavily affected clones may have to be discarded. However, a technique has been developed whereby when the minute apical tips of shoots of certain infected plants are cultured aseptically on nutrient media some of them grow into 'virus-free' plants. For instance Morel and Martin (1955), Holmes (1956) and Qual (1957) have been able to produce small healthy plants of dahlias, chrysanthemums and carnations respectively from infected clones. In 1955 Morel (1960) tried this technique with orchids and obtained healthy plants of cymbidiums from ones infected with mosaic virus; but instead of getting just one plant from one meristem, as had been the case with other genera, Morel observed that each meristem first developed into a mass of tissue morphologically similar to the protocorms which are often found when orchid seeds are sown in vitro (Curtis and Nichol, 1948). This protocorm-like body may then develop a shoot and roots or it may divide into two or more masses or it may produce several lateral protuberances (Morel, 1965). When these masses are cut into pieces each piece may proliferate again to give more masses, which in turn are also capable of further proliferation or of developing into a plantlet (Morel, 1965). Later it was discovered that if the meristems were cultured in a liquid medium and particularly if this was kept constantly in motion the number of protocorm-like bodies could be greatly increased (Wimber, 1963 and 1965). From one isolated meristem many plantlets can therefore be obtained. When, for example, the cutting-up process was repeated on three occasions and each time the pieces were transferred into a fresh nutrient medium and cultured again several hundred plantlets were obtained (Wimber, 1963).

Morel (1965 a, b) estimates that if frequent cutting up of cymbidium protocorm-like bodies could be successfully continued throughout a period of one year four million plants would be obtained from one meristem! When no further cutting up is done and the protocorm-like bodies are transferred to a solid medium plantlets develop.

That was copied from the paper and it should be clear to anyone interested that this has had a great effect on cultivation of cymbidiums. But there is one parallel defect. It

Meristems are grown in flasks in the same way as seedlings and are usually transplanted into fresh flasks when they reach this stage.

is possible that both hybridising and the cultivation and propagation of cymbidiums suitable for the hobby and outdoor cultivator may be discontinued, and the cult will be the poorer for that. The names and dates in parentheses in the quoted material refer to particular publications by the various experimenters which have been completely summarised by the authors of the Nottingham paper.

If either seedling or meristem propagations are bought, it should be just before the start of the growing season so that the small plants may be repotted into the common mix used in the rest of the collection. They should be established and in active growth in a few weeks. If bought out of season or at the wrong end of the growing season it will almost invariably result in a halt and setback, unless they happen to drop into a congenial home.

It may be asked, what proportion of a collection should flower each year? Allowing for those which are shy and all other factors such as propagation and repotting, a good average would be 50 per cent. In some years it could be as high as 80 per cent, in others as low as 40 per cent. But there is no reason why repotting should interfere with flowering. Some allowance should be made however for the lack of quality on such plants as have been repotted and later flower.

The use of artificial heating to force flowers seldom pays off. Apart from probable ragged opening sequences on spikes, it can cause bud drop. The greatest influence on the plants is climate. A little thought on this point soon discloses that, in spite of widespread use of heating in cooler climates, cymbidiums mostly flower earlier where the climate is good and no artificial stimulus is used. If early flowers are wanted, for either commercial production or to spread the flowering season out a little, plants, seedlings and meristems should be selected for this purpose, rather than trying to force the plants to do what they are naturally disinclined to do. It will always be found that the flowering of individual clones is not precisely dated each year. They may be treated in exactly the same fashion each year, but the flowering time or the opening of the buds may vary by as much as two or three weeks.

While this book is more about growing cymbidiums than flowering them, the end product is what we all look forward to, not the plants themselves. The use of heating or climate control in glass-houses, however, should be aimed at plant cultivation more than controlling or assisting flowering, as this will follow on normally from good growing practices. A good simile is that of a factory where the components are manufactured and collected by the day staff and assembled into finished products by the night staff. This may seem off-beam to the outdoor and ordinary grower, but it applies just the same. The sunlight, water and food are the things the plants work with during the day, but the flowers are made at night, even if they are dependent on prevailing weather patterns.

It is scarcely possible to outline a cymbidium growing calendar, because the timing varies so much from place to place. At best the outline would go as follows for a general cultural program, starting in the spring, by repotting all those plants which need it; shading and looking after these convalescents with a little more individual care than those carrying on; repotting again in January as carefully as possible if it seems it would do a little good; looking for flower spikes on the early cymbidiums about the middle of February, followed by a scan over the others about the end of February. After the beginning of March and slackening of the growth process, be careful that the plants are not overwatered; attack all the pests which would eat the flower spikes if they had a chance; give the plants a thorough once-over for virus and if any are found isolate them, and later destroy them if they confirm the fears. Spraying for scale, red spider and other pests, including a spray for brown rot, should be applied at least twice in the growing season October to March. Mostly the plants look after themselves quite well, all that the grower contributes are the things they would get if they were growing naturally, like water and fertiliser. Perhaps the perceptive grower will add quite a few things to that list because, after all, the grower is the one who makes the things happen, not the people who write books.

# Diseases and Pests

All growing plants attract what we call 'pests' and orchids seem to attract more than their share. They are as much parts of nature as the plants, but we have to discourage them as much as possible. For some this is easy, but not for others. The worst of them is the scourge of virus infection and there is little we can do about it. Cleanliness is the best counter, extending from culling infected plants to sterilising equipment. This includes all the tools used, the pots in which they are grown and, if taken to the ultimate, the potting medium in which the plants grow. Visitors should be discouraged from running their finger and thumb up or down the leaves, a pastime which seems irresistible to many. Above all, if everyone stopped selling infected plants it would be a very good lead-up to perhaps controlling the infection rate in some measure.

Virus infection takes on many appearances in orchids, but the most common in cymbidiums is, first, the lack of color in patches and spots on the leaves, sometimes called chlorosis, and the final stages when the chlorotic patches and spots turn black. It is not correct to label all the chlorotic spots and patches on cymbidium leaves as due to virus infection, as there are other causes. In orchid culture the common name 'mosaic' is used to designate the disease, more particularly when it is verified by the necrotic or black markings and spots.

There are sufficient indications of a link between tobacco virus and that which affects cymbidiums to discourage use of tobacco by a grower, or the constant sterilisation of the hands before having anything to do with the plants. Tobacco virus is not destroyed in the manufacturing process and one of the strange twists to that is, although the tobacco crop may appear to be free of infection, it apparently carries the virus and is immune to its bad effects.

In between the definite indications of virus infection are other aspects such as poor chlorophyl distribution in the leaves, giving rise to light patches which later disappear, red-brown staining of the immature leaves, zig-zag streaks of chlorosis, and red-brown staining and even black areas on new growths, which may be caused by any one of a number of things.

Although other orchids are affected, these are the usual things visible on cymbidium leaves. Sometimes it is a rather hard decision to make, but most growers with large collections do not hesitate to burn suspect plants. They will have no plants with leaf discoloration at all, particularly if they grow commercial or export flowers.

Virus-infected plants usually show traces of their illness in the roots as well as the leaves. When the roots are broken they have black layers under the epidermis or outer skin, and at times the whole root is discolored. Healthy cymbidium roots are light colored and when broken are white, green or creamy white inside.

If you wish to give them another chance, always isolate the suspected plants, particularly if they are expensive propagations. If the symptoms become pronounced and the flowers themselves show discoloration, or black spots where the color should be clear, it should be assumed that the plant has virus and should be destroyed. Many orchid growers still have infected plants in their collections, some even selling them instead of destroying them. When buying plants, resolution should be shown when offered suspected plants and a refusal given, or at least an understanding that if it turns out to be virus the plant should be replaced or money refunded.

In theory, the visual cleanness of plants should be sufficient, because that is all we can go on. But, in some forty years of experience with cymbidiums, I have my own ideas. In the first place, I believe that every cymbidium raised since the 1930 era has a susceptibility to virus, most of them carry the virus but only a minor proportion exhibit the symptoms to such a degree that they are useless as commercial flower producers or show-bench subjects. A simple parallel to this is the existence of the influenza virus and the way it affects human beings. Most people will be able to follow it from there without amplification of the idea. So far, no one has come up with a cure for either the cymbidium virus or the influenza virus, although many have tried.

No one can say with certainty how cymbidium virus is spread, but there is sufficient evidence for a reasonable suspicion that the chief point of entry is through the root system, rather than anywhere else. If that is accepted, it will be realised why emphasis is placed on cleanliness in the glass-house. This extends to all the implements and even to the pots. They should be passed through a wash of disinfectant or sterilised in a large container if they are re-used. There is no certainty that this will totally prevent infection and perhaps means a lot of trouble for smaller growers, but it is worth while if expensive propagations are bought. And what about the outdoor grower? Despite the fact that such plants are a lot hardier than glass-house-grown plants, suspected virus carriers should be passed out and replaced with clean ones.

The section on propagation outlines what can be done in the way of raising clean meristems from infected clones. If so wished, a bulb of an irreplaceable cymbidium should form the basis of a virus-free clone, although it may take some time to get it. In the meantime, there is good reason to isolate and cultivate such a plant. There is always the possibility that it may need a second try and a definite possibility, too, that the clone may be one of the visually apparent cymbidiums which will always show it is a victim.

Frequently, disease is blamed for flower defects but there seems no real basis for this. Occasionally, flowers carry color breaks or darkening of pigment in irregular patches, large or small, where no such color should occur. While sometimes due to disease, at other times it is simply inability of the plant to properly control color owing to its uneven chromosome make-up. Some authorities maintain that all color breaks are virus-caused, but this may be incorrect.

Where black spotting appears on the buds, and later on those parts of flowers not exposed before the flower opens, it may be due to virus infection which is not apparent on the foliage. If this spotting or discoloration persists over a period, it is almost certain the plant is a virus carrier, and it may infect other plants if handled at repotting. It should be discarded with those visibly infected. The leaves are the real indicators and usually so unmistakably affected that there is little risk that a non-virus infected plant is being discarded.

While virus seldom is severe enough to destroy a plant, another of the few diseases affecting cymbidiums can do so very quickly. It is usually called 'brown rot' and its severity seemed to coincide with introduction of what is known as the Westonbirt strain. It seems wrong to saddle this group with all the ills which beset the cymbidium grower, but unfortunately the breeding line seems to have a lower immunity level than the original first and second generation hybrids. It could be allied to the chromosome instability of the group as a whole, attributable to inbreeding as much as anything else. Brown rot is caused by a fungus spore either the same as or similar to that which attacks stone fruit in humid weather. In most instances the infection is primarily on the leaves, but the major damage occurs at the junction of the leaves with the pseudo-bulbs. The first indications of the pest in the glass-house or on the plants is the appearance of wet-looking brown patches on the tips or any section of the leaves, which later turn black as that section of the leaf is killed. There may also be a slightly sweet smell of the infected area, just as though the sap in that part of the leaf or bulb is fermenting.

Treatment consists of keeping all the leaves dry and infected parts of the leaves or pseudo-bulbs should be painted with any of the anti-fungus preparations; such as Captan, Capthion, Natriphene, Zineb, or any of the other anti-fungicides or copper derivatives available from nursery suppliers.

Complete protection is possible by using sprays before the disease gets into the plants in the first place. The spray should be applied as routine culture about the beginning of November, preferably after the repotting is finished, and again at three-monthly intervals. It should be applied on a cloudy day and early in the morning. Most of these sprays can be used at any time of the year and some of them are systemic, that is, they are absorbed into the plant tissue. Although brown rot can affect plants at any time of the year, it is more frequently found in conditions of high humidity and low temperatures. With sprays applied at intervals, the active agent is washed down into leaf axils and stays there, preventing to a large extent infections in that area.

Brown rot is a wind-borne infection by spores, which attach or blow on to wet or moist areas and soon enter the plant tissue. In glass-houses or roofed structures, it is a good idea to spray the underside of the roof twice a year when spraying the plants. This kills off the spores which grow in the condensation on the glass or in the overlaps of the roofing material. Plastic or fibreglass single-sheet lengths used in roofing should also be sprayed, because the spores are there even though invisible.

Once attacked, the leaf is permanently marked. If near the tip it may be cut away with a sterilised pair of clippers or a sharp knife. If the bases of the leaves are affected they should not be stripped from the pseudo-bulb, but after spraying or painting the affected areas they should be dried off and watched for recurrence. There is usually a small section of the enclosing leaf base which remains green and this keeps the leaf functioning even when most of its base is blackened and useless.

Occasionally the same infection, or a similar form, may enter the cut surfaces of the rhizome and work its way through the plant, killing it quickly and without much surface indication. Cymbidiums bred along the green lines seem more affected than other colors.

Any drastic shrivelling or leaves turning yellow-green should be suspected as an indication of rhizome rot. In most instances if the bulbs are squeezed low down, and the disease is present, a squashy one will be found. The plant should be immediately removed from the pot and examined to see if any of it can be saved. The possibility is remote, but even a back-bulb is better than no plant at all.

If a knife is used it should be sterilised each time a cut is made and the plant dissected until a clean section of the rhizome or a bulb is found. This salvaged piece should be thoroughly painted where the cut was made, using any of the anti-fungicides or a mixture of lime and a fungicide.

The infected rhizome is easily distinguished because it shows up with brown discoloration of the fibres or the sap. In bad infections the whole of the rhizome will look like the rotten wet patches which appear on the leaves.

Good ventilation in all weathers no doubt will allow spores of many undesirable things like brown rot to enter the glass-house, but routine spraying will stop them from getting a hold. Plants also should be kept a little drier in cooler weather to stop moisture remaining on the leaves. Ventilation will prevent condensation on the leaf surfaces, where brown rot most frequently gets its start.

Distorted flower buds are frequently caused by using sprays intended to get rid of red spider or ants, or any one of a number of other pests. The buds should never be sprayed with anything other than water and if a pesticide is needed the spikes should be covered with newspaper envelopes taped on with adhesive tape. Frequently, in late spring, particularly on warm days, red spider can move in from the garden very quickly and the only way to deal with it is by spraying. After spraying, the paper envelopes can be torn off and the spikes should suffer no harm.

Flower spikes are a great attraction to aphids, but there is no way they can be dealt with by spraying pesticides. They must be removed manually and treatment started

81

outside the glass-house. The source should be fairly easy to locate — a rose bush starting grow or some other sappy plant or shrub — and this should be cleaned up to stop the invasion of the glass-house. Mostly aphids get inside the bud cluster before it starts to open out and will usually be found on the underside of buds where they cannot be seen. All the spikes should be gone over about once a week.

Earthworms should be discouraged in cymbidium pots, as they eat their way through the decay portion of the mix, ejecting it again as fine soil which turns to mud when the plants are watered. A week or so after repotting, a top-dressing of lime should be sprinkled on and watered through. It quickly discourages the worms and is more beneficial than otherwise for the plant. Outdoor plants should be limed twice a year. It is also not beyond the bounds of possibility that earthworms could be virus carriers, as they live on the decay materials which form so much of the potting medium.

Few pests eat the leaves of cymbidiums but several attack the flower spikes and the flowers. Slugs and snails are most destructive, but they can be controlled by using baits, powders and sprays which contain the chemical metaldehyde. Do not rest on the fact that the baits, powders or sprays have produced a 'kill', because both these pests invade again very quickly. The treatment should be part of complete cultivation, because it appears at times that, if slugs and snails can get a good drink or wash of water, they shed the poison and recover. Baits should be scattered frequently. The flower spikes should be doubly protected. If show-bench plants are grown, a thick pad of cottonwool should be wrapped around the stem and dusted with powder metaldehyde. As spikes of exhibition plants are not sprayed or watered, this is enough to give adequate insurance. It is impossible to treat spikes in commercial glass-houses or large collections in this way, so the 'specials' should be picked out and so treated, while looking after the others with a bait-scatter.

Woodlice, or 'slaters' as they are known, are mobile pests which do little harm to cymbidiums, although they do invade the drainage holes and base of flower pots. They will eat the roots but are not as destructive as some of the other pests. They should be kept out of the glass-house as they multiply rapidly if allowed a foothold. They can be got at with contact sprays or common slug and snail bait which has been pepped up with Lindane. Like aphids, treatment for woodlice should be started outside the growing area by getting rid of their hiding places — stacks of pots, piles of timber, heaps of rubbish, or anywhere else which is moist and has rotting vegetable matter. They mostly live at ground level.

Many types of sprays have been used by orchid growers over the last forty years and so far as is known they have been used with few ill effects. No doubt many were used carelessly, at times with materials as lethal as any known poison where a couple of drops were enough to kill a person. A number of these sprays have been banned from general use, but their use as pest controllers in flower crops should not have been affected. At times the effect on the environment was quoted, but in an enclosed place like a glass-house, where the environment is self-contained, it should still be possible to use some of the banned formulations.

Invasions of ants into a glass-house have to be experienced to appreciate what pests they are. There are only two sprays which control them effectively, DDT and Dieldrin, both of which are banned for general use in many parts of Australia.

For the summer pests that never seem to die out, such as red spider, any one of the systemic sprays should be used as a matter of routine and as the effectiveness wears off it should be reapplied. There are several of these sprays obtainable at nursery suppliers and it is advisable to use them a little less strongly than outlined in the instructions, making up for the strength with more frequent applications.

Red spider is usually a sign of aridity in glass-house cultivation and, if it shows up, a little higher humidity should be aimed for by watering the benches and paths more frequently. It is an underside sap-sucking insect which cannot be seen by most people with the naked eye. The leaves of cymbidiums take on a silvery appearance when attacked severely. If the leaf is turned over and examined it looks finely speckled, and there is a minutely filmy web woven over the underside. In ideal conditions red spider multiplies rapidly; it can cause bud deformity and completely ruin flower spikes once it attacks them. It can be hosed off flower spikes if found early enough. When hosing the spikes, look inside the sheaths on the stems because that is one of the spots where it can be missed, and is frequently found.

Red spider has been blamed for the spread of virus from one cymbidium to another. While this is a possible source of cross-infection, it is a minor one. Even where there is no red spider the virus has spread to a considerable extent. Red spider usually attacks weaker plants first, or seems to do so, spreading later to those which are better able to supply sap. If sprays for red spider are used, they should be applied with an upward jet under the leaves to get contact as well as absorption if the spray is systemic.

'Smoke bombs', as they are called, are manufactured by ICI Chemicals and are available at most nursery suppliers. They may be used instead of sprays but are not as effective. If they are used, all the ventilators should be closed, the bomb farthest from the door lit, then following up the glass-house toward the door, closing it as the last one ignites. The glass-house should remain tightly closed for up to an hour. After opening the door, do not go into the glass-house for about another hour or so until the air clears, open the ventilators and leave again. Do not stay inside for any length of time until the following day. To control spider, these bombs are far more effective when combined with spraying.

Whatever sprays or smokes are used, wash face and hands after handling and use, and wear an old plastic overall coat to cover ordinary clothes. Any contact with the skin should be avoided; if made, it should be washed off immediately and not after the job is finished.

In some ways the outdoor grower of a few plants has an advantage, because natural control exists over most pests and only those which eat the plants or flowers, like slugs, snails, caterpillars or woodlice, need to be acted against. Red spider has a natural humidity check and the various fungus infections have only a minor effect, such as occasional brown leaf tips or a patch or two on other leaf surfaces in cold and humid weather. Outdoor plants seldom suffer as much from brown rot as those grown indoors.

Southern states do not get many flying pests, apart from egg-laying moths. Where prevalent, Dendrobium beetle will attack cymbidium spikes and there is little that can be done about laying a trap for this pest. The only cure is a pair of sharp eyes and a heavy foot. The caterpillars which emerge from the eggs laid by moths and butterflies also pose this problem and can only be countered in the same way, possibly when it is too late.

Scale is one of the pests which attacks epiphytic orchids more frequently than terrestrial genera like cymbidiums. If it makes its way into a glass-house it will probably be the common mussel scale, which looks just like a tiny half-shell of these moluscs. Strangely, it seems to be the green cymbidiums again which get it first, as in the case of red spider. The same type of systemic sprays used for red spider will prevent scale getting a foothold and, at the same time, its entry is usually brought about by ants. Keep the ants out and the scale is usually kept out, too.

Perhaps we should end this section with a summary, in the same way as the other sections of the book. It is short but appropriate:

All too frequently the first plants bought by inexperienced growers are diseased or of poor quality. This is regrettable, because it turns away so many from orchid growing, particularly cymbidium growing, which can in reality be so easy. While, at times, it may be an unscrupulous commercial grower who does this, all too frequently it is ordinary cymbidium growers who know what they are doing. Selling infected plants is a way of cutting the loss which would be incurred if the plants were put where they rightly belong, in the incinerator.

It may be a different thing giving away a plant known to be diseased and telling the recipient that it is so and should be used only as a means of finding out if it can be grown, and later destroyed if it proves the point.

Plants which have blemished foliage should not be sold or bought, or even offered as a gift, unless in the instance outlined in the last paragraph. Most of these certainly, are virus infected and represent a poor start to orchid growing.

If sprays are used, take all reasonable precautions against inhalation as well as skin contact. Some people are more susceptible to ill effects from various sprays than others, but do not approach the process of applying sprays with fear. Handle the materials wisely and carefully.

It is always best to attack the pests, insects and other harmful things, by supposing that they are already there, rather than wait for them to do the damage and then attack them.

Typical virus-infected leaves compared with a clean leaf. While originally the markings may be white or pale green spotted, these areas soon turn black as the foliage ages. The leaf in front of the two virus-infected leaves has been injured at the tip first by brown rot and then finally by the plant dehydrating to a degree where it starts to cast leaves and die back on the newer ones. It is a summer phase aggravated by original cold-humid fungus infection and the leaf, if on a good plant, should be cut back to within 3 mm (⅛ inch) of the green part.

The roots of virus-riddled plants are usually also affected. As this photograph shows most of the root is black and discolored with only two growing tips moving to support the plant. While the black root is also partly active, its role is very restricted. There is no cure for such plants and unless good reason can be given for retaining them in a collection they should be destroyed. The condition can be minimised by good culture, but they always present a risk to the rest.

The central pseudo-bulb of this propagation indicates the devastation caused by brown rot infection of the leaves and leaf bases. In this instance the infection has been spread by watering the spores of the fungus down into the leaf axils, where it has quickly reduced almost the total leaf base to dead tissue. While it can be halted at this stage, there is no chance of the bulb maturing and flowering as would have been expected. Usually this is a glass-house hazard not so pronounced outdoors.

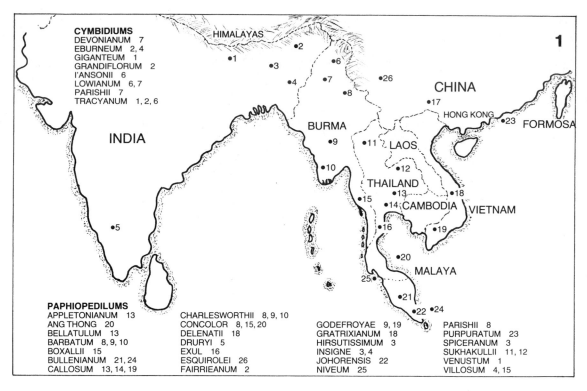

**CYMBIDIUMS**
DEVONIANUM  7
EBURNEUM  2, 4
GIGANTEUM  1
GRANDIFLORUM  2
I'ANSONII  6
LOWIANUM  6, 7
PARISHII  7
TRACYANUM  1, 2, 6

**1**

HIMALAYAS
CHINA
HONG KONG
FORMOSA
BURMA
INDIA
LAOS
THAILAND
CAMBODIA
VIETNAM
MALAYA

**PAPHIOPEDILUMS**

| | | | |
|---|---|---|---|
| APPLETONIANUM  13 | CHARLESWORTHII  8, 9, 10 | GODEFROYAE  9, 19 | PARISHII  8 |
| ANG THONG  20 | CONCOLOR  8, 15, 20 | GRATRIXIANUM  18 | PURPURATUM  23 |
| BELLATULUM  13 | DELENATII  18 | HIRSUTISSIMUM  3 | SPICERANUM  3 |
| BARBATUM  8, 9, 10 | DRURYI  5 | INSIGNE  3, 4 | SUKHAKULLII  11, 12 |
| BOXALLII  15 | EXUL  16 | JOHORENSIS  22 | VENUSTUM  1 |
| BULLENIANUM  21, 24 | ESQUIROLEI  26 | NIVEUM  25 | VILLOSUM  4, 15 |
| CALLOSUM  13, 14, 19 | FAIRRIEANUM  2 | | |

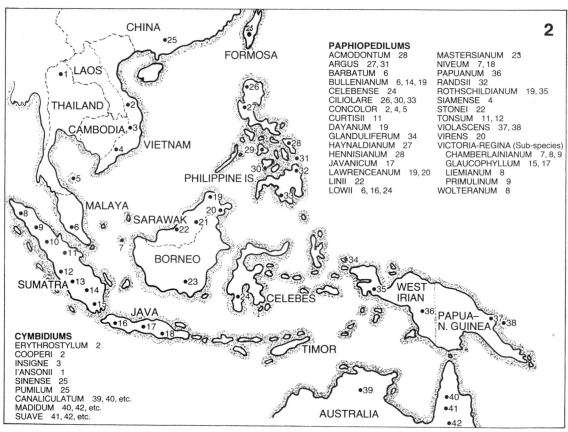

**2**

CHINA
LAOS
FORMOSA
THAILAND
CAMBODIA
VIETNAM
PHILIPPINE IS.
MALAYA
SARAWAK
BORNEO
SUMATRA
JAVA
CELEBES
WEST IRIAN
PAPUA– N. GUINEA
TIMOR
AUSTRALIA

**PAPHIOPEDILUMS**

| | |
|---|---|
| ACMODONTUM  28 | MASTERSIANUM  23 |
| ARGUS  27, 31 | NIVEUM  7, 18 |
| BARBATUM  6 | PAPUANUM  36 |
| BULLENIANUM  6, 14, 19 | RANDSII  32 |
| CELEBENSE  24 | ROTHSCHILDIANUM  19, 35 |
| CILIOLARE  26, 30, 33 | SIAMENSE  4 |
| CONCOLOR  2, 4, 5 | STONEI  22 |
| CURTISII  11 | TONSUM  11, 12 |
| DAYANUM  19 | VIOLASCENS  37, 38 |
| GLANDULIFERUM  34 | VIRENS  20 |
| HAYNALDIANUM  27 | VICTORIA-REGINA (Sub-species) |
| HENNISIANUM  28 |   CHAMBERLAINIANUM  7, 8, 9 |
| JAVANICUM  17 |   GLAUCOPHYLLUM  15, 17 |
| LAWRENCEANUM  19, 20 |   LIEMIANUM  8 |
| LINII  22 |   PRIMULINUM  9 |
| LOWII  6, 16, 24 | WOLTERANUM  8 |

**CYMBIDIUMS**
ERYTHROSTYLUM  2
COOPERI  2
INSIGNE  3
I'ANSONII  1
SINENSE  25
PUMILUM  25
CANALICULATUM  39, 40, etc.
MADIDUM  40, 42, etc.
SUAVE  41, 42, etc.

**Map 1**

This map of localities of occurrence of species cymbidiums and paphiopedilums is neither complete nor strictly accurate. It is intended to give some idea of the localities and countries where these orchids occur. In most instances a species will occur in small isolated pockets in certain areas and varieties may be found many kilometres from the site of the original discovery. Map 2 should also be referred to.

**Map 2**

The number of species shown on this map is incomplete and there is little doubt that many habitats of paphiopedilum species are yet to be discovered. In some instances, such as that of Papua-New Guinea and perhaps other islands, the knowledge of both habitat and certainty about nomenclature are unclear. Map 1 should also be referred to.

**Map 3**

The phragmipediums of South America are perhaps better known in their countries of origin than in collections. This map also is incomplete and inaccurate, serving only as an indicator of the countries in which most of the species occur. Information on the actual habitats is very sketchy, frequently noting an area which does not appear on any available map as the point of origin.

**3**

GUATEMALA
●1

COSTA RICA ●11
PANAMA ●12

●2
VENEZUELA

●3

●4 ●5
COLOMBIA

●2A GUIANA

●6
ECUADOR

●9

●7

●8A
PERU

●8

BRAZIL

●13

●9A
BOLIVIA

●10 ●

ARGENTINA

CHILE

URUGUAY

**PHRAGMIPEDIUMS**
CAUDATUM   1, 2, 6, 8, 12
KLOTZSCHEANUM   2, 2A
LINDLEYANUM   2, 2A
STEYERMARKII   2
SCHLIMII   3, 4
HARTWEGII   5, 6, 7
LONGIFOLIUM   4, 6, 10, 11, 12
CZERWIAKOWANUM   7
BOISSIERANUM   8A
CARICINUM   2A, 9, 9A
SARGENTANUM   10
VITTATUM   10, 13, etc.
CHICA   12

# Cymbidium Pedigree Charts

**CYMBIDIUM SENSATION** is typical of the line for breeding red cymbidiums. The involved species for this characteristic are *Cymbidiums insigne, i'ansonii* and *garnet*. It is unfortunate that *Cymbidium tracyanum* entered the pedigree, because it introduced a possible source of brown. This brown tinge is prominent in many otherwise good red cymbidiums, obvious in some clones of *Cymbidium* Spartan Queen. While the curious blending of so many species in 1970-80 cymbidiums gives a certain amount of unpredictability, hybridisers should line out their projects in pedigrees similar to these two examples before pollinating.

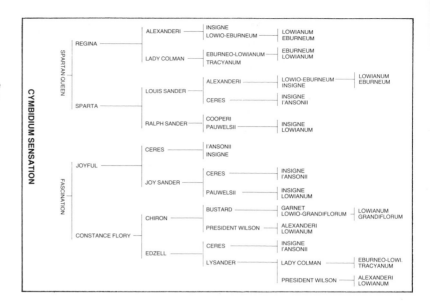

**CYMBIDIUM JUBILATION:** This grex showed a preponderance of yellow clones. While the lower half of the pedigree could be expected to give some green inheritance factors, the upper half proved dominant. In analysing this result a critical examination of the pedigree of *Cymbidium* Auriga could cause dissatisfaction and suspicion that it is inaccurate, while the lower half, extending the progenitors of *Cymbidium* Borough Green, illustrates a classic green line-breeding result. If duplicated it would breed true greens with occasional yellows, but perhaps lacking the shape characteristics imparted by *Cymbidium* Alexanderi through *Cymbidium* Balkis.

These two charts contain all the elements for combination of the species into hybrids of all colors from white through to deep red, from green to deep golden yellow. *Cymbidium erythrostylum* should preferably appear for early flowering characteristics.

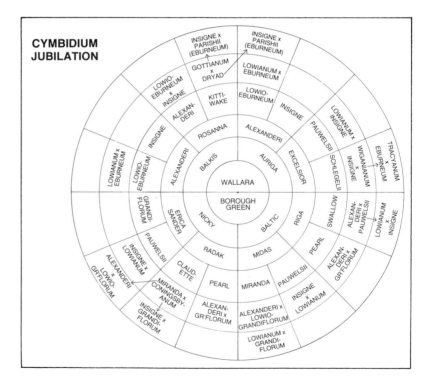

PAPHIO. INSIGNE, probably the variety *sylhetense,* frequently grown as a windowsill plant indoors and occasionally flowering as such. It grows much better under glass-house conditions.

*Far left:*
PAPHIO. INSIGNE var. SANDERAE is the mutation of the commoner type form, and there are several other similar mutant forms of this orchid catalogued.

PAPHIO. SPICERANUM was frequently found growing in the same area as *P. insigne* and early imports of bulk lots of the two species occasionally included natural hybrids between them.

PAPHIO. INSIGNE plant showing a sport or mutation similar to *P. insigne* var. *sanderae.* It would be a chance in a million, this one occurring at a Victorian orchid nursery.

*PAPHIO. INSIGNE* var. *HAREFIELD HALL,* possibly originally known as variety *montanum* or *giganteum,* the habitat of which, still a matter of uncertainty, was denuded.

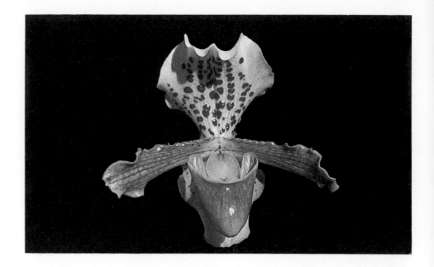

*PAPHIO. VILLOSUM,* from Burma and at one time other parts of north-eastern India, is one of the hardiest of the species, originally found growing as an epiphyte in large trees.

*PAPHIO. BOXALLII* was generally regarded as a variety of *P. villosum,* although from a totally different area of Indo-Asia. Its flower is not as large as that of *P. villosum.*

PAPHIO. CHARLESWORTHII is one of the most beautiful of the species and it is little wonder that demand for it always exceeded the supply. At one time it was freely grown in Australia.

PAPHIO. CHARLESWORTHII in a much paler form. These two examples illustrate almost the extremes in coloring, with the paler varieties always appearing to have a rounder outline. This species was reintroduced by American hybridists in the late 1970 decade with very good results.

PAPHIO. BARBATUM, with P. charlesworthii, established a red blood-line which contributed to most of the hybrids of that color. The petal shape was not persistent.

*PAPHIO. EXUL*, although remarkably similar to *P. insigne* in color and shape, originated in an area a considerable distance away. The flowers are long lasting and glossy. First flowered by Richard Measures in England in 1892.

*PAPHIO. FAIRRIEANUM* is unusually colored and the shape is singular for the part of India where so many members of the genus occur. Varietal naming of this species is perhaps overdone.

*Far right:*
*PAPHIO. CURTISII* var. *SANDERAE*, like its counterparts within the *insigne* and *callosum* complex, fitted in very well with the visionary hybridists and they took it into the craft together with the mutant form of *P. lawrenceanum. P. curtisii* var. *sanderae* appeared in a batch of plants consigned to Sanders about 1910. It gained a First Class Certificate from the RHS in 1915.

*PAPHIO. HIRSUTISSIMUM* has never been a popular species in cultivation, although it is accommodating in the matter of fitting into collections of various orchids in a way uncommon to the genus.

92

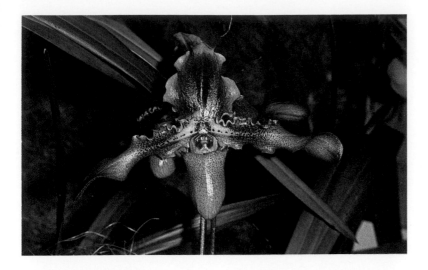

*PAPHIO. ESQUIROLEI,* a species from southern China for which there is little information, easily identifies itself with *P. hirsutissimum,* a native of the India-Burma border areas. In this it has similarity to the *P. victoria-regina* group, with superficial overall resemblance but sufficient distinction to give impressions of speciation rather than separate status.

*PAPHIO. CALLOSUM* is one of the most beautifully colored of the species but the overlong, drooping and persistent petal shape did not fit in with hybridists' wishes.

*Far left:*
*PAPHIO. LAWRENCEANUM* has more red toning than *P. callosum,* but the two are remarkably similar. Both have beautiful foliage, perhaps better than that of many house plants grown for this feature.

*PAPHIO. TONSUM* is closely related to *P. lawrenceanum* and *P. callosum,* but is not mentioned in the text. It was brought into cultivation about 1880, again imported with another species.

*PAPHIO. VENUSTUM* is one of the color jewels of the species. While it had this distinction in addition to being 'the first' species cultivated, the hybrid list eclipsed it for many years.

*PAPHIO. BELLATULUM* was originally found growing in the same area as *P. charlesworthii* and the two produced natural hybrids which puzzled early growers of the genus for some time. *P. bellatulum* was subsequently found in several other areas.

*PAPHIO. NIVEUM* usually has a longer stem than its relative *P. bellatulum* and the sparse spotting led to hybridising for white Slippers. The habitats of the two are completely separate, although they appear to have many common features.

94

*PAPHIO. CONCOLOR,* like *P. bellatulum* and *P. niveum* and many other species Slippers, originated in limestone sections of country and this natural habitat background can be extended into artificial culture with good results.

*PAPHIO. PAPUANUM* is a discovery of the 1960 period, but the name and status of this Slipper and one or two closely resembling it are yet to be fully determined. The flower illustrated could be a form of *P. violescens* or a member of a linked group such as the *P. victoria-regina* sequence of Java and Sumatra, or it may be accepted as *P. bougainvillianum.*

*PAPHIO. PURPURATUM* was originally thought to be solely native to the island of Hong Kong, but there is good reason to believe that it grows also on the Chinese mainland in a rich orchid area adjacent to Vietnam.

95

*PAPHIO. GODEFROYAE.* This illustration is a reproduction of a lithograph from about 1890. Before color photography many artists used orchids as their subject material and although at times they took licences with facts, in general their reproductions were both elegant and artistic. The printing was perfection itself.

*PAPHIO. ACMODONTUM* was a fairly recent addition to the catalogue at the time the book was produced. There is valid opinion to substantiate the claim that it is a variety of *P. ciliolare,* an orchid which is subject to frequent misleading identification. If further proof of this is needed it is necessary only to refer to the English *Orchid Review* over the years 1893 to the present time. One of the failings of identification is lack of understanding of the variation of species.

*PAPHIO. SUKHAKULII* was found, as so many other orchids have been found, growing with another species Slipper, in this case *P. callosum,* in northern Thailand in 1964. It is closely related to *P. wardii,* which grows in northern Burma, and is a mottled foliage species needing warmth to grow well.

96

*PAPHIO. HAYNALDIANUM* belongs to a distinct group of long-petalled Slippers which bear the closest resemblance to their distant relatives the phragmipediums, of Central and South America. Adventurous hybridists in the later years of the 1960-1980 period have a lot of new material to work on, much of which, like *P. haynaldianum,* has relatively unknown potential.

*PAPHIO. PARISHII* was discovered in Burma about 1860 and is possibly the least cultivated of all the species. The foliage is the thickest of all the Slippers and the flowers, which occur together on the spike and up to four or five in number, are long lasting. While some clones are colorless, others are in shades of pale to deep red-brown, sometimes purple-brown on green background.

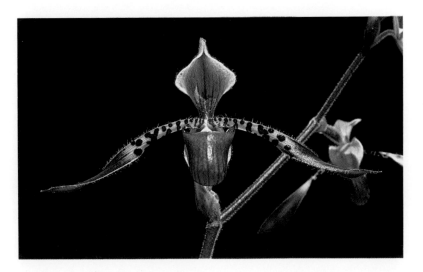

*PAPHIO. LOWII* is found in several countries and there is little variation in the flowers from different localities. While it is cultivated more for its color than other features, the color potential has had little work. Preoccupation with shape in paphiopedilum hybrids had the effect over more than 100 years of encouraging rejections and accounted for the enormous list of hybrids.

97

*PAPHIO. ROTHSCHILDIANUM* has been responsible for the production of many orchids such as this supposed hybrid. Like *P. parishii*, *P. rothschildianum* is rare in cultivation. It was brought into collections about 1880 to 1890 in a cloud of deception and misrepresentation as well as shady identification and concealment of its habitat.

*PAPHIO. ARGUS,* from the Philippine Islands, took its name from the Greek god of a thousand eyes – the reference point being the numerous spots which cover the petals. The flower measures about 7 centimetres across. The Greek gods are well represented in the hybrid list, as scarcely one genus does not have at least one representative of the pantheon.

*PAPHIO. GLANDULIFERUM* (synonym *praestans*) has only one recorded habitat. The long petals are neatly folded in the buds and it is an experience to see the flowers open, the petals unfold, extend to their full length and then twist. Naturally the time lapse is a full day to two days, but it can be followed quite easily with a camera.

98

PAPHIO. MASTERSIANUM, from Borneo, has the tessellated or marbled foliage common to so many of the Slippers of that area. Usually taken as a sign for warm cultivation, it is not an infallible guide, as some of them originate at high altitudes where the climate is quite different from that of the lowlands.

PAPHIO. WOLTERANUM belongs to a small group of Slippers with the same purple-tinged petals as *P. hirsutissimum*. Most of the group have very long stems considering the flower size, developed probably because of the habitat being immersed in higher surrounding herbage.

PAPHIO. SIAMENSE is apparently a natural hybrid between *P. callosum* and *P. appletonianum* and is usually found growing with *P. callosum*. At first it was thought to be a new species and was named *P. sublaeve*. It has somewhat similar foliage to *P. callosum*, though slightly narrower.

*PAPHIO. LINII* is from the strangest of all habitats, the humid mangrove swamps of the north coast of Borneo. On appearance it also is related to *P. appletonianum* and the hooded dorsal sepal seems to always assume an almost horizontal position. It is not an easy Slipper to cultivate in a mixed collection of other species.

*PAPHIO. CURTISII* was named after Charles Curtis, one of the proteges and collectors associated with the Veitch establishment in the 1870 period. Curtis sent this Slipper back to Veitch from Sumatra in 1882. It grew at about 1000 metres (about 3500 feet), but likes warm conditions in the glass-house. The picture is taken from an old lithograph of the 1890 period.

*PAPHIO. APPLETONIANUM,* native to Thailand, has the long stems common to members of the group. Its existence in its habitat is under threat from the same common causes which affect all the remnants of orchid species. Remnants is probably the only word which fully describes the sparseness of their occurrence in the later stages of the twentieth century.

*PAPHIO.* HARRISIANUM (*P. barbatum* x *P. villosum*) was the first hybrid registration in Sanders' list of Slippers, although it was not the first hybrid raised. Many unnamed and unknown parentage cypripediums, as they were then known, were involved in the preliminary sort-out. The variety illustrated, Ball's, is one of the best ever produced.

*PAPHIO.* CROSSIANUM, named in 1873 some four years after *P.* Harrisianum, is the second accredited hybrid. It is from the cross-pollination of *P. insigne* and *P. venustum,* which was one of the first species introduced into England. Its effect on subsequent generations of Slipper hybrids is minimal, unlike that of *P.* Harrisianum.

*PAPHIO.* LEEANUM was the final weld of species Slippers which was to have such a dramatic effect on the future. It occurred as a natural hybrid among batches of species imported into England from India and these plants aroused much speculation because of their foliage before the flowers appeared.

*PAPHIO.* LATHAMIANUM (*P. villosum* x *P. spiceranum*), although not as important for the future as some of the other primary and secondary hybrids, still had some part to play. It is undoubted that the hybridists and growers of the time did not appreciate just how far their initial efforts would be taken. The modern Slipper grower is hard pressed to keep up to developments.

*PAPHIO.* REDSTART brought into the line a later addition with *P. charlesworthii* and without its influence there is some doubt that the red genes in other species such as *P. barbatum* would have been sufficient to give us the red characteristics apparent in the late years of the twentieth century and even much earlier. Its parentage is unknown, which is unfortunate.

*PAPHIO.* PAEONY 'Regency' is one clone of this hybrid which has been outstanding as a parent. It is from the cross-pollination *P.* Noble x *P.* Belisaire, the latter having as one parent *P. bellatulum.* The short stem of this species is apparent in *P.* Paeony and often disadvantages growers of the clone. However, good growers produce a moderate stem of up to 20 centimetres.

102

*PAPHIO.* ORCHILLA 'Chilton' provides evidence of the potential of *P.* Paeony and probably reflects most closely the wishes of hybridists for a rounded out-line with good color. This flower when photographed was two months old.

*PAPHIO.* NOELLE CLAIRE 'Picardy' (*P.* Condia x *P.* J. J. Heaton) displays the same shapely characteristics in a flower which follows a completely dif-ferent line to *P.* Orchilla. The spotting is a direct inheritance from *P. insigne* through about ten generations and the dividing line on the petals from the species *P. villosum.*

*PAPHIO.* THULE 'The globe' follows a different line again with green coloring probably from *P. spiceranum* in the petals, the spotting from *P. insigne* in-tensified in the petals. Many of these shapely Slippers prove sterile or very difficult to breed with. Sometimes reversing the pollen parent induces fertility.

*PAPHIO.* DIVERSION 'Picardy' is the inbred descendant of *P. insigne* var. *sanderae* and one of the few clear light green Slippers to appear in many years of breeding. It is probably capable of furthering the line provided similar parents are selected, as it goes back to Christopher, one of the famous antecedents of so many modern hybrids.

*PAPHIO.* LEMON HEART, if left to its own devices, is one of the best yellow Slippers. Yet when shaded correctly it has almost as good a color as *P.* Diversion. It also goes back along the same lines to *P.* Grace Darling and so to *P.* Christopher. But, like *P.* Diversion and so many other famous modern Slippers, it also goes back into unknown parentage dead-ends.

*PAPHIO.* F. C. PUDDLE owes its whiteness to four species Slippers – *P. bellatulum, P. niveum, P. spiceranum* and *P. insigne* var. *sanderae.* Although small, it so impressed the RHS Orchid Committee that it was awarded a First Class Certificate and probably still is the whitest hybrid in the catalogue.

*PAPHIO.* SWANILDA (*P.* Bradford x *P.* F. C. Puddle), although larger than its white parent, has already lost some of the whiteness. Criss-crossing the breeding lines may still get a reversion to almost pure white, but so far the linkage has not been properly solved.

*PAPHIO.* COPPERWARE (*P.* Sharon x *P.* Hellas) is a direct follow-through of the colors of the species *P. villosum, P. boxallii* and *P. insigne* var. *sanderae.* It is a twelfth generation hybrid with an elaborate pedigree and qualifies the prediction of the raiser of *P.* Hellas, Mr H. G. Alexander, that Hellas would have an impact on Slipper breeding.

*PAPHIO.* GAYSTONE (*P.* Blondell x *P.* Tafelrose) is a similar follow-through to *P.* Copperware, but in this instance the color line has gone through the genes to a dominant green instead of gold. Although there is some similarity in the different clones of one cross-pollination, at times some surprising results accentuate the inclusion of so many different species in the one flower, with occasional lapses where reds should dominate.

*PAPHIO.* MAUDIAE 'Magnificum' (*P. callosum* var. *sanderae* x *P. lawrenceanum* var. *sanderae*) is a natural result from what we call two albino parents. Both were pale green and white mutations of usually colored species and, like albino·cattleyas and several other constant types of orchid species, breed true to the mutation so long as the line is followed.

*PAPHIO.* GOULTENIANUM was bred from the type form of *P. callosum* and *P. curtisii,* giving a most beautiful combination of colors in a quite different shape from the types which win most of the prizes and awards. These colored Slippers add feature points to collections which, if confined to award-type flowers, seem to have a sameness about their members.

*Far right:*
*PAPHIO.* HEATHER MIST (*P. barbatum* x *P. victoria-regina* sub-species *glaucaphyllum*) is not the type of hybrid which gains ready acceptance in the circle intent on award features, but it indicates perhaps the inquisitive mind reappearing after the lapse of nearly a century. Such cross-pollinations are the source of surprises in some instances.

*PAPHIO.* INVINCIBLE was bred from the species *P. hirsutissimum,* from which it has its beautifully colored petals and soft olive green dorsal. Like so many of the primary or secondary hybrids, it is relatively easy to grow into a specimen plant carrying up to ten or twelve flowers. The other parent of Invincible was Monsieur de Curte (*P. boxalli* x *P. insigne*).

The hybrid *P.* Perseus x *P.* Londinum was never named and perhaps the reason lies in the time it took this clone to flower. From the cross-pollination to flowering was about twenty-four years, eighteen of which I spent cultivating the seedling. While it grew fairly well, it never formed a flower bud in that time. The same failing applies occasionally to other genera.

*PAPHIO.* RED KNIGHT was named in 1940 and gained an Award of Merit from the RHS Orchid Committee in England. While possibly not the best red Slipper ever raised, it is nevertheless quite good and could have been expected to in turn create a good follow-on breed. It had failings, apparently, because little has followed it up to 1980. But one day compatible partners may be found to perpetuate its beauty.

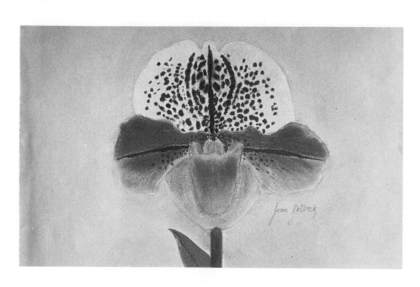

*PAPHIO.* GRAND MONARCH was one of the largest Slippers ever raised, with a dorsal sepal about 12 centimetres (5 inches) across. Despite the stoutness of the flower on its 30 centimetre stem, it was a poor grower, failing always to propagate more than one growth at a time even when an old back-cut was possible. Even stranger, it is not registered in Sanders List of Orchid Hybrids. This pastel drawing from a black and white photograph was colored fairly accurately from memory.

107

Orchid growers all have their own potting mixtures based on experience and blended to suit their conditions. This photo shows the real test and it should be taken each year at the end of the growing season, when the root system has reached its full development. Penetration should be complete, with the tips either sealed off or active. Rot at the tips indicates that dormancy has been reached and the plant over-watered or perhaps overtaken by a cold spell and too low a temperature.

These four Slippers have been consolidated under the title *P. victoria-regina* as sub-species, a logical classification based on their appearance. This phase in their cataloguing represents taxonomy at work. The word frightens some people and the exponents of its use sometimes annoy others. In this instance it concerns orchids which were discovered by various people in different localities and subsequently dealt with separately. Possibly the latest member to gain notice was *P. primulinum* on its rediscovery after many years. They are all natives of Indonesia. One of their attributes, apart from their color and general attractiveness, is the elongating flower stem producing buds for up to six or more months in good cultivation.

Clockwise from top left:

*P. chamberlainianum;*

*P. glaucophyllum;*

*P. primulinum* forma *purpurascens;*

*P. liemianum.*

108

**PHRAGMIPEDIUM LONGIFOLIUM**
should on appearance alone combine with several of the paphiopedilums for hybridising purposes, but although the barrier appears to have been penetrated for more than 100 years cross-pollinations have been tried without success. These Central and South American orchids grow in similar conditions to their Asian counterparts and should be part of the Slipper grower's collection.

PHRAGMIPEDIUM SEDENI (*Phrag. longifolium* x *Phrag. schlimii*) was one of the early hybrids in the genus and some of its varieties are most beautifully colored. One of the attractions for modern hybridists, of course, is the beautiful pink coloring which they seek to take into an inter-generic cross. Unlike many other genera, inter-generics between paphiopedilums and phragmipediums seem hard to initiate. The only pink source for hybridists in paphiopedilums seems to be the species *delenatii,* from which French breeders have produced some good colors.

PHRAGMIPEDIUM SCHLIMII was discovered in Colombia in 1867 by Schlimm, an orchid collector of that period and sent to England and the European centres. The English firm of Veitch and Sons seemed to specialise in the genus and one of their growers named Seden worked to advantage on them. *Phrag. schlimii* grows up to about 1500 metres, but prefers cultivation in a warmed glass-house. This is a particularly good colored form of the species, most of which are rather drab.

PHRAGMIPEDIUM CALURUM is the hybrid between *Phrag. longifolium* and *Phrag.* Sedeni. Having only a few members in the genus, the phragmipediums are much inbred, most of the hybrids having appeared early in their history as cultivated orchids.

PHRAGMIPEDIUM SCHRODERAE
(*Phrag. caudatum* x *Phrag.* Sedeni)
was one of Seden's hybrids which
flowered first in 1883. It was named after
Baroness Schroder, the wife of one of
the notable orchid growers of the day,
later famous in cymbidiums as the re-
gistrant of *Cymbidium* Remus. *Phrag.*
Schroderae varies considerably from
clone to clone, some having quite long
petals. The species *Phrag. caudatum* is
a most difficult subject to photograph, as
its petals are at times some 60 to 80
centimetres long.

The two Slippers, *P. Colonist*
'Wellington' *(top)* and *P.* Joviella
'Moorilla', represent the type of flower
still being bred after some forty years'
progress in the genus. In fact, they still
reflect the same configuration of color
distribution and shape achieved in the
1930 period. Perhaps qualification
could be given to that by admitting that
throughout the range of any one cross-
pollination brought to flowering, there
would be a greater percentage of this
type of flower, with the cull rate lowered
to a great degree. But despite this, if any
improvement is to occur in the future of
Slippers it will apparently need to be
induced by inter-generic hybridisation
or introduction of breeding lines derived
from cross-pollinations of some of the
smaller members of the genus and a
reworking of past cross-pollinations.

*PAPHIO.* SEVERN x MEGANTIC, raised more than forty years ago but never named, almost marked the total development possible from the original species and was possibly never visualised by the hybridists working on the first and second generations of the genus. The objects have not changed almost from these very early days — a rounded outline the most important, with good color and strong, vigorous stems. The leaves of the hybrid *P*. Severn x *P*. Megantic were extremely thick and very wide.

*CYMBIDIUM MADIDUM* growing as an epiphyte in the old butt of an enormous elkhorn fern in a coastal swamp area in northern New South Wales. The plant is about 2 metres in diameter and about 6 metres from ground level. This is the largest morphologically of the Australian cymbidiums but with possibly the smallest flowers.

*CYMBIDIUM EBURNEUM* appears to be related to other species in the Indo-Asian area in a way similar to the paphiopedilum species complex of *P. victoria-regina,* with environmental and ecological effects apparent in minor overall differences in evolution. The time scale could only be a guess.

A single flower of *Cymbidium eburneum,* showing the pink tinge in the column, the golden keels of the inner labellum surface and the pale yellow splash of color on the central lobe, commonly inherited in hybrids removed many generations from the primary hybrids.

*CYMBIDIUM LOWIANUM* growing as a garden plant. It is among the hardiest orchids and can be grown in a raised rockery or as a potplant under light shade trees. While not frost tender, the leaves and flowers could be considerably affected by severe conditions. *Cymbidium lowianum* seldom fails to flower, but the spikes never appear on the new growths, only on fully matured bulbs of the previous growing season. This characteristic is inherent in hybrids but is met on equal terms by the propensity of other species to flower on the newly maturing pseudo-bulbs. The flowers of *Cymbidium lowianum* are long lasting.

*CYMBIDIUM LOWIANUM* occurs in many varieties, ranging from almost golden-yellow monochrome to very dark bronze-green forms, red-bronze tones and even a variegated mutation. In most instances the red-brown vee of the labellum is constant.

113

CYMBIDIUM INSIGNE, like *Cymbidium eburneum,* is morphologically different from other Indo-Asian species because the pseudo-bulbs are usually rounded instead of ovoid and tapering to a peak. It is seldom seen in cultivation and is shy to flower unless the pot is full. Most of the plants of *Cymbidium insigne* were stripped from their habitats and most of those so exported have been lost or destroyed. Considering the mutilation of Vietnam, the home of this orchid, little can remain of its once profuse orchid population.

CYMBIDIUM LOWIANUM var. *PITT'S* was an unusual form imported into England toward the end of the nineteenth century. It was much used in hybridising, but most traces of its use have been lost. However, some of it is still apparent in the modern yellow hybrids of the 1970-80 decade. (Pastel drawing by Joan Skilbeck.)

*Far right:*
CYMBIDIUM GRANDIFLORUM is possibly the only consistent colored species among the members of the larger flowered Asian group. While the size may vary a little and the spotting of the petals become more intense in some varieties, the labellum and color are constant. The yellow hybrids of later generations owe quite a lot of their size and color to the influence of this cymbidium.

CYMBIDIUM TRACYANUM is the 'straggly' member of the species. The petals and sepals seem to fall away from the centre of the flower, but the spikes arch nicely and the flowers are always well positioned. Like *Cymbidium grandiflorum,* the warmth tolerance of *Cymbidium tracyanum* is low and the flowers quickly drop if a warmer than average day occurs. Its season is consistently followed and it is usually the first of the species to flower. Unfortunately its breeding potential is limited, but its influence is still apparent in some of the better colored hybrids.

114

*CYMBIDIUM TRACYANUM* growing as a garden plant, a role it fills quite well. As it usually flowers about the beginning of May, it is a welcome addition to the early winter flowers. Tolerant to the point of hardness, *Cymbidium tracyanum* sends its flower spikes up with the new growth in sometimes the hottest summer months. If given mostly speckled shade and an occasional watering these spikes grow quickly, but naturally will be better with a little care and some fertiliser.

*CYMBIDIUM* LOWIO-GRANDIFLORUM, named about 1900, was an early hybrid, but not the first. Much hybridising was carried out in other genera before the potential of cymbidiums was realised somewhere about 1910. Just as combinations of the species in the Slippers produced an amazing array of hybrid flowers from cross-pollinations, the cymbidium species also established a tremendous heritage of color.

*CYMBIDIUM* PAUWELSII (*C. lowianum* x *C. insigne*) was a combination of two important species that led to much of the vigor and color of cymbidium hybrids. This is a pastel of the variety 'Comte de Hemptinne' raised early in the twentieth century. Like *Cymbidium* Alexanderi 'Westonbirt', it was a chance tetraploid, but not the only one from this cross-pollination. Like most hybrids, some growers had the propensity for bringing out the color in this clone and while some considered it a drab thing because they could not handle it properly, others produced such as the illustration.

*CYMBIDIUM* PEARL 'Magnificum' (*C. grandiflorum* x *C.* Alexanderi), with *Cymbidium* Pauwelsii 'Comte de Hemptinne', were a magnificent pair of early hybrids. While many of the early hybrids were somewhat 'stringy' in appearance, the use of outstanding parents led to the development of better flowers by selective hybridisers. The breeding lines established had the potential for further development which is illustrated in some of the other color photographs. This pastel drawing is based on a black and white photograph colored in conformity with the description of the flower when it gained an award of a First Class Certificate in 1930. It was a very large flower, but in those days the measurements were not given.
(Pastel drawing by Joan Skilbeck.)

*CYMBIDIUM* REMUS FCC (*C.* Regulus x *C.* Joyful) remained a closely guarded secret apparently for some years. Competition in the flamboyant days of orchid growing was no less keen than at any other period and at times false parentage was recorded for hybrids to prevent copying by other breeders and fanciers. This reacted against itself because it was so common as to be a nuisance and a mischief. *Cymbidium* Remus comprised several clones, but the FCC variety was the most outstanding and had significance in color breeding which will always carry through for as long as the genus is cultivated. This also is a pastel drawing. *Cymbidium* Remus was flowered first some time in the 1930 period.

*CYMBIDIUM* RIO RITA 'Radiant' (*C.* Pearl x *C. ruby*), although another 1930 period hybrid and not a large flower, is a follow-on from *Cymbidium* Pearl which has marked out a place for itself possibly in the list of immortals. The hybrid lines, while selected for improvement which shows out particularly in those of the 1970-80 period, will need these early hybrids again to stiffen the breeding lines. Compared with the later hybrids the petals and sepals of *Cymbidium* Rio Rita may seem a little pointed, but its beautiful coloring and the labellum are the things which are used for perpetuation of good flower characteristics.

*CYMBIDIUM* WOLLAR 'Sandra' (*C. Balkis* x *C.* Remus) is a beautiful example of the development and blending of cymbidium bloodlines. The sepals of this flower were 5 centimetres (2 inches) across, the petals about 4.25 centimetres. It was an outstanding clone from a good series but it was prone to disease although a strong grower and for this reason did not survive. It was a virus victim; the best cymbidium seedling I ever bought and flowered.

*CYMBIDIUM* GIRRAHWEEN 'Enid' in the 1945-55 decade set a standard which has since become commonplace and, in fact, has been superseded. There were several clones in the Girrahween complex, which were among many seedlings sent to Australia at the outbreak of the second world war. There has always been some doubt about the given parentage, *Cymbidium lowianum* x *Cymbidium* Flamenco, and considering the haste and worry of a dispersal in a place like Sanders, it is possible that a misnaming occurred, not the first and not alone in the thousands of plants sent hither and thither in the world even today.

*CYMBIDIUM* BALKIS 'Patricia' appeared in Australia about the same time as *Cymbidium* Girrahween. In fact, there were three separate clones which were indistinguishable. The cross-pollination of *Cymbidium* Alexanderi 'Westonbirt', x *Cymbidium* Rosanna 'Pinkie' has been repeated several times and some outstanding clones have been produced. *Cymbidium* Balkis is without doubt the most outstanding cymbidium ever produced up to the 1970-80 decade, as the illustrious list of its seedlings will demonstrate.

117

*CYMBIDIUM* ALEXANDERI
'Westonbirt', naturally, was the beginning of all the development seen over the years. This remarkable cymbidium, which had so few flowers yet so much potential, was a chance seedling noted by the man after whom the hybrid was named, Mr H. G. Alexander. Unfortunately, this clone seems to be prone to virus attack, but since its quality was appreciated most hybridists have had to live with this fact. Even the meristem process, although it produced virus-free plantlets, was not sufficient to cure the susceptibility. This is a pastel impression of a cymbidium as notable as its offspring, *Cymbidium* Balkis.

*CYMBIDIUM* ROSANNA 'Pinkie' (*C.* Alexanderi x *C.* Kittiwake) was perhaps the beginning of the sequence as one of the parents of *Cymbidium* Balkis. This somewhat inbred little group often suffered criticism in their offshoots because of lack of color, however much they made up for it in shape. *Cymbidium* Rosanna, of course, was another milestone in the career of H. G. Alexander. Strangely, although it could be expected that the Rosannas would all be tetraploid cymbidiums if the variety 'Pinkie' was so, in fact some of them were quite sterile. (Pastel drawing by Joan Skilbeck.)

*CYMBIDIUM* WALLARA 'Gold Nugget' was among many later hybrids to negate the criticism levelled at the Alexanderi and Balkis hybrids. Interestingly enough, all that beautiful golden yellow can be traced back to two species – *Cymbidium lowianum* and *Cymbidium tracyanum,* of all things! Provided, that is, the pedigrees really are as stated. I always had a suspicion that more than these two were responsible and that tucked away into the breeding line somewhere was also the species *Cymbidium grandiflorum.* In its turn, *Cymbidium* Wallara is having great effect in line as a pollen and seed parent.

118

*CYMBIDIUM* BOROUGH GREEN 'Opal' also owes its color to *Cymbidium lowianum* and *Cymbidium grandiflorum*, but the tinges of color which just edge the green are also a follow-through from the species *Cymbidium lowianum*. These tinges at times are used as a means of discounting an almost perfect flower by standards pursued to their illogical conclusions. Color is never a perfect thing in nature, always owing its existence to the contrasts provided to show it up.

*CYMBIDIUM* WALLACIA (*C.* Warona x *C.* Alnwick Castle) is a large flower and traces back to the combination of the colors of four species – cymbidiums *lowianum, insigne, grandiflorum* and *eburneum.* The progenitor *Cymbidium* Sussex 'Laelia Sasso' was the crucible where they were all melted down and fused, and the breeding lines following through from this cymbidium are typified in some of the other illustrations. *Cymbidium* Wallacia is a larger, better colored descendant of *Cymbidium* Sussex, and almost identical. The vee pattern of the red labellum had only one source, *Cymbidium lowianum.*

*CYMBIDIUM GWENDA* 'Leonore' follows a similar color breeding line to that of *Cymbidium* Wallacia, but the labellum of *Cymbidium* Balkis intrudes quite clearly. This type of labellum appears to be a combination of the red *Cymbidium lowianum* vee with the negative *Cymbidium eburneum* labellum. In some flowers it almost indicates the labellum discoloration following pollination of cymbidium flowers and at one time led to rejection of such flowers for the export market and penalising by judges under the award system.

Two hybrids from the last years of the 1970-80 decade were developed by Alvin Bryant of Sydney, one of the leading world hybridists of that period. The background is *Cymbidium erythrostylum,* which has poor petal stance in the developed flower. They jut forward. American hybridists working on this species chanced on a tetraploid form of *Cymbidium* Earlybird, which traces back through *Cymbidium* Edward Marshall to *Cymbidium insigne* and *Cymbidium tracyanum.* Both Cymbidiums *tracyanum* and *erythrostylum* are early flowering and formed a good basis from which to work. From *Cymbidium* Earlybird the American hybridists got *Cymbidium* Stanley Fouraker and so to *Cymbidium* Winter Fare. In these latest hybrids, *Cymbidium* Winter Fare x Valley Paradise *(top)* and *Cymbidium* Winter Fair x Fanfare, appear two lines which give this type of flower in June-July, something breeders and growers alike had been seeking, in order to get away from the poorer type of flower available until their advent.

*CYMBIDIUM* KATHIE LOVELL was produced by an Australian breeder named Duncan and *CYMBIDIUM* SLEEPING BEAUTY represents another facet of the Alvin Bryant touch on the genus. These pure-color cymbidiums owe their place in the catalogue to *Cymbidium lowianum* var. *concolor* more than to any other species. However, the genes for producing the monochrome labellum and flower came to dominance over a considerable color background and represent the result of good parent choice.

CYMBIDIUM SYLVANEERA reaches almost the utmost potential for size in hybrids. The parentage of these two clones is *Cymbidium* Keera x *Cymbidium* Sylvania 'Sonnet' and it is along these lines of large open-type flowers that what are known as the 'export type' flowers are bred. Color was very much considered at one time and 'stripey' type flowers were discarded in favor of clear colors. However, expanding markets and buyer education have changed that into acceptance of a large range of colors, even to the bizarre.

CYMBIDIUM FAIR PROMISE at 12 centimetres (5 inches) across represents about the maximum development of size possible in the genus. The plant's capability to build and support such a spike is also limiting the number of flowers borne on it to a few unless a build-up morphologically to pseudo-bulbs about twice the usual size accompanies the process. So far this has not occurred and the size of the bulbs has remained practically unchanged from such early hybrids as *Cymbidium* Ceres.

CYMBIDIUM OVATION (*C.* Sussex Dawn x *C.* Parma) proved to be one of the most consistent hybrids over all in color and shape that appeared in the 1970-80 decade. *Cymbidium* Sussex Dawn is a proved green breeder and many other outstanding cymbidiums were bred from it. Green cymbidiums may be bred at will, but most of the other colors are a chance because of their mixed color breeding lines.

*CYMBIDIUM* BEXLEY RADIANCE *(top)* and *CYMBIDIUM* SENSATION 'Cecil Park' in this quality of flowering represent the nearest to clear red so far achieved in hybridising cymbidiums. Again the colors stem from the original species sources of *Cymbidium i'ansonii, Cymbidium tracyanum* and *Cymbidium ruby,* apparently with the catalyst of *Cymbidium* Lowio-grandiflorum – a green cymbidium – so prominent in each of these two bright flowers.

*CYMBIDIUM* NGAIRE 'June' has the white bordered petals and sepals which probably originated in *Cymbidium giganteum. Cymbidium* Ngaire has a double line of the species cymbidiums *giganteum* and *ruby,* with the border firmly anchored among its genes.

*Far right:*
*CYMBIDIUM* CLARISSE CARLTON (*C.* Cambria x *C.* Babylon) carries the genes for large spikes of flower from its progenitor *Cymbidium* Pauwelsii. Before cross-pollinations, hybridists should always go through the routine of tracing the proposed parents. In this way, although the colors may be elusive, the good or bad habits of the preceding generations can usually be selected or discarded.

122

*CYMBIDIUM* WINEGROVE (*C.* Sussex Pearl x Sensation) came from orchid breeders noted for color – Wondabah of Sydney. Usually when a good colored cymbidium is used to breed further into denser colored reds a reversion is not only possible but quite frequent. While not a sure way to prevent the reversion, using a breeding line strong in green cymbidiums stemming from the species *grandiflorum* can frequently assist in retaining color, if not intensifying it.

*CYMBIDIUM* HIGHLAND GLEN (*C.* Rio Rita x *C.* Babylon). This hybrid represents the cross-pollination of two of the most valuable breeding clones in the cymbidium catalogue. While not always a guarantee of success, good parents of proven breeding capacity are almost a necessity if hybridising is attempted. Cross-pollination and seed raising from poor stock is not only a waste of time and money, it clutters the bench until the stock is proved useless. Far too many amateur hybridisers start off the wrong way and waste years of their time.

*CYMBIDIUM* LUNAGRAD 'Elanora' has been one of the 'guinea pigs' of the orchid world. This picture shows two clones of the hybrid, one of which was treated as a small meristem propagation with colchicine, which affects the genetic and so the chromosome make-up of the growing cells. The difference between the two flowers is obvious, with the colchicine-treated clone showing larger and stouter characteristics.

*CYMBIDIUM PUMILUM* has been used in more miniature cross-pollinations than any other small cymbidium and although in some instances the green color of the albino variety prevails, at other times color breaks through. Its disadvantages are forward jutting petals and pendant, short spikes.

*CYMBIDIUM ILLIBERALE* is a Formosan species with plenty of color. It grows at about 2000 metres in a warm, open environment on rocks. As a potential miniature hybrid possibility this small cymbidium has plenty to offer, particularly for a breed which may cope better with semi-tropical conditions.

*CYMBIDIUM CANALICULATUM* var. *SPARKESII* is the dark form of this Australian species, the largest flowered of the three Australian cymbidiums. It has proved difficult to use as either pollen or seed parent with standard cymbidiums and may one day prove to be a relative but not a true cymbidium. The type is usually green densely spotted with red-brown to purple-brown.

124

CYMBIDIUM SUAVE should breed neat miniature hybrids because of its thin, close-set pseudo-bulb system and very small purple-spotted flowers. In some flowers the green base color is densely spotted with red-brown. The feature of the elongating, frequently flowering pseudo-bulbs, if brought out in hybridising, would be a great asset.

Far left:
CYMBIDIUM DEVONIANUM, with its pendant spike of some thirty flowers, has been possibly the outstanding parent of the miniature series of the 1970-80 period. In particular the hybrid Cymbidium Bulbarrow is outstanding. (Pastel drawing by Joan Skilbeck.)

CYMBIDIUM LANCIFOLIUM, a Formosan species, is typical of a fairly large number of miniature Asian cymbidiums which are rather difficult to cultivate in artificial conditions. Their potential for miniature breeding has not been fully realised.

CYMBIDIUM MASTERSII is an easy species to cultivate and makes a noteworthy plant in an orchid collection. Its habit and the spike habit recommend it for cultivation in a slat or wire basket so that the flowers can be seen when they come out.

CYMBIDIUM ALOIFOLIUM, a Burmese species, has the longest spike of the pendant cymbidiums, growing up to 60 to 80 centimetres and with up to about thirty flowers. As the spikes are thin and wiry, there is little chance of training them to upright habits.

*Far right:*
CYMBIDIUM SWEET LIME (*C. Esmeralda* × *C. madidum*), far right, resulted from the rather belated use of the Australian miniature cymbidium species for miniatures. Although there is incentive to produce colored minis, until use of the greener varieties of the Australian species only *Cymbidium pumilum* was the source for greens. The trailing habit of *C. madidum* persists, even though *C. insigne* is in the background.

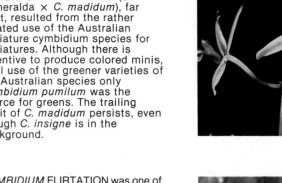

CYMBIDIUM FLIRTATION was one of the first of the modern miniature cymbidium tribe to appear, possibly inspired by H. G. Alexander's *Cymbidium* Minuet, one of the first to appear since about 1934. *Cymbidium* Flirtation is a *Cymbidium pumilum* hybrid from the colored type of that species; the other parent is *Cymbidium* Zebra.

*Far right:*
CYMBIDIUM BEACON FIRE (*C. pumilum* x *C.* Khyber Pass). Although this miniature has one of the best qualifications for cymbidium flowers, that of color, the habit of the flower spike is well illustrated here to the disadvantage of the clone. It is necessary to stand it on a platform to see the flowers and almost impossible to photograph it artistically.

CYMBIDIUM OLYMILUM (*C. pumilum* x *C.* Olympus) is the marriage between the large and the small which brought out the best of both types. While longer spikes of flower are preferable to lift the blooms above the foliage, if the plant form is also miniaturised the effect is just as good. Too many of the so-called miniature and novelty cymbidiums have foliage which does not suit either the name or the flower spikes.

CYMBIDIUM SWALLOW 'Lemon Beauty' is a step backward in time to the period of the war years of 1939, the haste of despatching orchids to safe places and the probability of a wrong name. This clone was an outstanding cymbidium in the post-war years, but if I were asked to give it a name it would be President Wilson. Not that it mattered very much, because it turned out to be a triploid and little use for breeding. Even as a 1970-80 cymbidium it would have a lot to recommend it.

CYMBIDIUM CHARM 'Elegance' was an outstanding colored cymbidium from the 1945 period, usually the first or among the first hybrid cymbidiums to appear in late May or June. The parentage was subsequently disputed. It is registered as Cymbidium Ceres x Cymbidium erythrostylum, but reference to English breeders in later years brought the opinion that it was really a clone of Cymbidium Sunrise. As most cymbidium growers come to realise in their later years, it is never wise to be dogmatic about something which cannot be proved.

CYMBIDIUM I'ANSONII remains a mystery species still, but there is little doubt that it appeared in Cymbidium Charm in some way. This color dominance, perhaps unduly credited to Cymbidium i'ansonii when some of the credit should go to others, must, however, stem from some common ancestor perhaps far back in the history of the genus and so long as cymbidiums are bred in red color lines the genes will show out.

127

*CYMBIDIUM* DIGNITY 'Barbara' is a
seedling from *Cymbidium* Charm. The
white line around the petals and sepals
is still there, the shape a little better and
the color of the labellum one of the
attractions. The change in cymbidium
shape over the years is the more remarkable characteristic as it was sought
to take the pointed tip off the petals and
sepals and give them a rounded effect.

*CYMBIDIUM* ALEXANDERI 'ALBUM'
is a series of steps backward along the
trail of cymbidium breeding. But this almost insignificant cymbidium had a very
important part to play in what are known
as pure-color cymbidiums. It is a relic
from the early part of this century, in-
heriting its purity from *Cymbidium
eburneum* and *Cymbidium lowianum*
var. *concolor.*

*CYMBIDIUM* ARCADIAN SUNRISE
'THE LIP' is among a number of
premier-type yellow cymbidiums which
have appeared in greater numbers than
other colors in the 1970-80 period. Why
yellow should be so paramount is not an
easy question to answer because there
was no real yellow species cymbidium
from which to inherit the color. Two obvious sources seem to be *Cymbidium
lowianum* var. *concolor* and
*Cymbidium grandiflorum,* with its green
conversion factors. *Cymbidium*
Arcadian Sunrise 'The Lip' is about 12
centimetres (5 inches) across.

*CYMBIDIUM* DESIREE possibly could rank as one of the earliest Australian hybrids with a trend toward the characteristics of 'shape'. It was raised in Sydney by Norman Webster about 1950. This hybridist will be remembered by some of the older growers of the 1970-80 decade as an innovator in seed-raising techniques in Australia.

*CYMBIDIUM* LUCIFER was raised about the same time as *Cymbidium* Desiree. Although named by W. A. Service of Sydney, it was possibly raised by Andrew Persson, another Sydney innovator who had distinction in the field in that city. It was the hybrid between *Cymbidium* Carisbrook 'Florence' and *Cymbidium* Veronique 'Bullfinch', both colored hybrids, producing some of the darkest shades in some clones yet also producing this green clone. It is still my belief that the red trail lies through these green recessives like *Cymbidium* Lucifer.

*CYMBIDIUM* CARISBROOK 'Brick' had the red inheritance from *Cymbidium* Ceres 'F. J. Hanbury', but the clone used to create the Lucifers was almost dark chocolate-red. It is difficult to imagine, on looking at *Cymbidium i'ansonii,* that these colors were latent in it, brought out in part by the other side of the pedigree. Although considered by some hybridists a retrograde step, a return to the Ceres bloodlines might provide a similar catalyst to produce that elusive clear red with the 'shape'. The Carisbrooks appeared about 1935.

*CYMBIDIUM* BOROUGH GREEN 'Conference' and *CYMBIDIUM* WALLARA 'Gold Nugget' are the parents of *Cymbidium* Jubilation. Photographed here together, they were used by Robert Hodgins of Frankston, Victoria, with almost the certainty that they would provide good material. Their pedigrees appear in another part of the book.

*CYMBIDIUM* JUBILATION is one of the best of the 1970-80 hybridisations, with the usual proportion of good and better in the seedlings flowered. Perhaps a disappointment to the raiser that a larger proportion were not shapely greens, it was a natural result stemming from the dominance of yellow as a color. Reverse cross-pollinations should always be tried when hybridising, preferably with the same parents and at the same time. This clone was not the best to flower in 1979.

*CYMBIDIUM* RIEVAULX 'Cooksbridge' indicates what could be regarded as the ultimate development of the labellum in this form. The whole flower represents a good combination of color while not conforming to the standards laid down for shape. Perhaps it could be said that too much emphasis is placed on the competitive potential of cymbidium flowers and too little appreciation given to their overall attractiveness. A wise grower blends the two and has much to show for his or her selectiveness.

130

*CYMBIDIUM* LEVIS DUKE 'Bella Vista' must rank among the best of the pastel green cymbidiums of the era and it is a far cry back to the narrow strips of green petal in the Cymbidiums *lowianum* and *grandiflorum* from which it has been developed. This plant was an exhibit at the 1979 Hobart Orchid Conference.

*CYMBIDIUM* WESTERN HILL was named by Russell Martin of McKinnon, Victoria; the result of his cross-pollination of *Cymbidium* Western Rose with *Cymbidium* Hamsey. It was the reserve champion cymbidium at the 1979 Hobart Orchid Conference, running second to one of the clones of *Cymbidium* Jubilation. It also must rank as close to the ultimate development of the genus.

The hybrid *Cymbidium* Western Rose x *Cymbidium* Mary Ann had not been named at the time this was printed, but it also is a Russell Martin hybrid from McBean's Orchids at McKinnon. This clone has flowers 12 centimetres across and a large and well-colored labellum. It also poses the question as to how much further breeding potential is available in the genus, either in color or shape and finally size.

Paphio. insigne

**Part 2**
*Slippers*

# Paphiopedilums

Hybrid paphiopedilums, although bred from species originating in all types of climate from cool to tropical, have developed into a stable order of plants which grow and flower best in a moist environment where temperatures do not fluctuate much outside the 12-20 degrees range. However, this does not bar them as orchids grown in controlled environments in much warmer climates. Control is fairly easy to achieve in double-glazed glass-houses or ordinary structures fitted with an inner liner of polythene film.

Some hybrids, as well as some of the species, are well suited to warm climates and those types should be selected for growing in warmer areas. They are bred from such species as *Paphio. callosum, Paphio. barbatum* and others originating from near-equatorial countries. There is plenty of scope outside that recommendation for growers willing to use a little ingenuity, although flower quality may suffer a trifle.

Originating in much the same area as the species cymbidiums, the paphiopedilums have been hybridised freely and the results from about the third generation are totally different morphologically from the species, a feature not nearly so pronounced or obvious in cymbidiums.

No particular genus of orchids may be singled out as easiest to grow, but in the light of years of cultivating them, I would select paphiopedilums because they are so consistently similar plants in the hybrid form. They do not blend particularly well into a mixed collection and a grower considering them should try to get this feeling, and resist impulses to mix them before mastering them. To some, they are a repulsive flower, but that also goes for other orchids as well.

A project with a lot to recommend it is building up a collection of species paphiopedilums. Such a collection should start off with the common ones such as *Paphio. insigne* varieties. Some of these plants would inevitably become problems because of peculiarity of habitats and general incompatibility. However, with a little more treatment as individuals instead of a general collection, there is no reason to doubt their ability to conform to a general cultivation program.

In 1968 the Royal Horticultural Society orchid committee decided to revert to the correct name paphiopedilum instead of the common term cypripedium, which rightly belonged to another genus. The derivation of the word cypripedium is from two Greek words bonded with a Latinised ending. The Greek words are *kypris* (Venus) and *pedi(l)on* (a sandal), which became the appendage 'pedium'. This name reverted to the terrestrial genus which grows in many countries of the northern hemisphere. The word paphiopedilum is also derived from two Greek words: *Paphia* (another name for Venus) and again *pedi(l)on*. Probably many of the generic names of orchids make the purists wince. The Central and South American members of the group are known as phragmipediums. The derivation here is also Greek, *phragma* a fence and again *pedi(l)on*. The fence is relative to the divisions of the ovary.

The genus we are concerned with are the paphiopedilums, and from here they may be variously referred to as such or as Slippers, the usual colloquial epithet. Phragmipediums, South and Central American orchids, species or hybrids, grow in the same conditions as Slippers and make a good addition to a collection.

As it is almost impossible to grow Slippers satisfactorily without a glass-house, the plan should begin with an existing one to be converted to the genus or building one to suit. It should be planned along the lines of those illustrated in the drawings, with a roof designed to take advantage of the best light. The walls may be taken to the roof or given a certain amount of what is known as side light. Side light is more a matter of construction preferences, as the bench arrangement can compensate.

If walled right up with brick or other material, the benches should be about half-way up the wall. If side light is built in they can be lower, which makes plant handling and inspection easier. The dimensions of the benches should be such that plants at the back are as easily reached as those at the front.

Ventilation should be arranged for installation of a fan system and perforated polythene tubing after the style advocated for cymbidiums, although this may be considered unnecessary. Various modifications of the system, with or without the tubing, are possible, even to recirculation of most of the air inside the glass-house. One section of roof ventilation should be arranged for each 3 metres of roof length, preferably at the apex of the roof and on each side, so that one side may be closed if necessary.

Ventilation of this order means that fairly rapid drying out could occur, but this can be counteracted by automatic foggers or vapor jets, in addition to the closed bench system with moist gravel or other aggregate as a base. The foggers are easily and efficiently controlled by a wet-leaf electrically activated system, details of which should be available from nurseries or horticultural equipment suppliers. One is illustrated.

A paphiopedilum plant has a fan-shaped form, with several leaves forming each fan or growth, new sections proceeding from the base of the fan or the rhizome. While the rhizome is distinct on some of the species, on others it is so short between the growths that it is almost non-existent. At times the plants grow in dense mats in their habitats. If the rhizome is examined it will be seen that it is nearly always of an ascending type and does not grow straight out from the last-made growth. It also has several growth 'eyes'.

The paphiopedilums have no pseudo-bulb system to tide them over poor periods and this is another indication of their position in the scheme of things. If in the past evolutionary years they had needed a pseudo-bulb system, they would have developed it like other orchids. It is surprising how drought-resistant they are. Their place is ground level or near it, where there is conservation of moisture and sufficient food to allow for a short root system to take it up quite easily. Naturally growing plants of such species as *Paphio. insigne,* for instance, may have roots up to 45 centimetres long when they grow in their habitat, but when grown in pots they conform to the shape of the pots and seldom exceed 25 centimetres, because the food and moisture are readily available. There is no need for the roots to extend to seek it.

Some of the species are epiphytic and lithophytic, some grow in masses of decaying vegetation almost at ground level. Few, if any, at any time grow in the earth as such.

Nearly all paphiopedilum leaves have an upper surface composed of a layer of clear cells which on some species, particularly those with tessellated or marbled foliage, gives them a most attractive crystalline appearance on well-grown, healthy plants. The depth of the layer varies from species to species, and, as the foliage is naturally conditioned to moisture, the leaves should be frequently sprayed. In good health they are always glossy.

The dense mat habit of some of the species is reflected in benching the pots so closely that they almost touch one another. The humidity generated in this way is the condition they prefer, rather than a plant or two scattered among a miscellany of other genera. The benching should preferably be closed, although this is far from necessary. If the bench is closed, additional humidity is easily conserved by a layer of moisture-holding material under the pots. A lip should be formed around the bench to hold about 5 centimetres or more depth of gravel, shell-grit, coarse sand, or small screenings.

The pots should be staged up from the front of the bench so that all the plants can be seen. This can be done in a number of ways and makes lifting plants out a lot easier, the leaves stand clear of adjacent plants in the tier in front and light penetration is better. Each tier of plants should be about 5-8 centimetres above the one in front of it. An easy way to arrange this is with 10-centimetre strips of fibro-cement sheet laid on a series of upended pots on the gravel or shell-grit base, or by any other convenient means. Fibro-cement sheet is pest and rot proof and easily cleaned.

Aspect of the bench to light source is fairly important and the benches should be so arranged that there are no dense shade areas or light pockets which would affect growth and flowering. Opinions differ about the positions of the plants relative to light source, and I have seen them growing well with full side light — as I once grew them — to positions some 75 centimetres to a metre below the top of the wall. Each aspect has its own peculiarities. If grown against a solid wall and well down in a glass-house they would occupy a natural position, but should be directly facing the light source. For the southern hemisphere the bench would be against the south wall and facing north for a good situation, with the plants tiered steeply against the wall.

A glass-house to suit this configuration would be any of the types illustrated, but should run east and west. For a glass-house with glass sidelights the bench may be facing any direction, the plants still tiered up toward the back of the bench, but less than if facing north and backing on to a wall.

There is no real advantage of one type of building over another, as a side-lighted house has excess light screened out by heavier shade-cloth or extra coats of paint. If asked to express a preference, I would settle for walls to roof style on account of simplicity of construction. A lean-to style, however, should have side light. With experience it will be found that although light intensity is a critical factor, good general cultivation determines plant health and flowering more than any single factor such as light.

Although it is better to position a glass-house to suit the genus cultivated, it is seldom possible in a suburban backyard to get everything right. Shade from adjacent trees and buildings is not as important when growing Slippers as when growing cymbidiums, which are better with unrestricted light. Go back to considering their respective natural habitats for confirmation of that.

The type of glass-house should be considered relative to the light source. Going back to the Slippers benched against a wall, it is possible to look at a suburban backyard and almost state with certainty what sort of orchids should be grown and in what type of glass-house, but that may not suit all the people involved.

Where a glass-house can be built on an unrestricted open space the choice is much wider than when a confined area is to be used. The various types should be considered and the best choice made. In all instances the closed bench has more to recommend it, because Slippers do not need nearly so much air circulation as epiphytic orchids or cymbidiums. In a small glass-house 3.5 metres long and 2.5 metres wide, it is possible to grow up to 200 Slippers and that is quite a good collection for a moderately small grower. An advantage of a glass-house this size is in lower heating costs.

Temperature control is important to stabilise growing and flowering Slippers as, although they are a mixture of several species, the individual peculiarities of these are long submerged in the general production of what could almost be termed a totally different orchid. While there is no truth in the theory that they should follow the pattern set in their beginnings in flasks of culture medium, the atmosphere should never approach the chill below 10-12 degrees. Doubtlesss there are many growers who will do better than that, but in looking for a reasonable applicable rule it is better to settle for something a little above average than below.

Locality has a lot to do with temperature control and while Slippers can be conditioned to take lower temperatures occasionally, it should not run into a pattern of days and nights. This is one of the areas where some divergence of opinion on minimums occurs.

Density of shade should be related to the intensity of the sun where the Slippers are

*Paphio*. Oakoira about 80 years from seedling, a good red color, still cultivated, 1980.

grown. While some growers will advocate light shade, others will find it totally out of phase for their plants and they may need to get back to the hand test, where a hand held about 30 centimetres above a sheet of white paper should not cast a shadow with correct shading. It is unwise to accept another grower's assessment, but make the shade adequate when starting out and see that, if shade-cloth is used, the foliage does not take on a light green or yellow-green look.

It is sometimes an advantage to use shade-cloth inside a glass or fibreglass roof rather than outside. The light intensity could have as much as 20 per cent difference with the same ratio of shade-cloth. While this may increase the inside temperature in hot weather, it can be corrected by installing a ventilation fan with an intake on the cooler side of the glass-house.

The color of fibreglass or corrugated plastic sheeting used on a glass-house roof is important. Although some authorities recommend that blue should never be used, it has been used quite successfully. However, it would be better to settle for pale green, opaque white or clear or uncolored fibreglass corrugated sheet roofing, each of which should be summer shaded to suit the area for Slippers.

Glass-house heating of any sort is expensive, but rather than buy a collection of good quality Slippers and try to grow them in below-standard conditions, it is better to settle for the less expensive species and hardy hybrids if the bills are going to frighten a grower off. Even in better climates, such as occur in sub-tropical latitudes, the temperature drop will have considerable influence on the type of flowers produced. Automated boosters which take care of sudden or occasional drops below a pre-selected minimum are a good investment, even if they hold two or three degrees above the absolute minimum. Upper limits are about 24 or 25 degrees, but an occasional day or so above that figure will do little harm if the glass-house is conditioned by ventilation and humidifying.

If a closed bench system is used, the bench filling should be sprayed frequently to maintain wetness. If an open bench system is used, the underneath strata should be kept wet, even if a floor covering of wood chips, tan bark or any other absorptive material is used. If the floor under the benches is earth it should be kept saturated and not allowed to dry out. This is the sort of environment the species were used to in the habitats; the forest, mountain gully or jungle areas where they originated. A continuation of that, while it may not sound so necessary, is at least some way toward following their life pattern.

One phase of their environment would be missing, for many of them stage through a fairly dry period of the year, which is largely unnecessary in artificial cultivation. Most hybrids will have a period through their cycle, however, where they will give indications that they are dormant, and it is possible to notice these plants and respect their periodic growth and recess habits.

The futility of advocating all sorts of fixed criteria for growing Slippers, or any other orchids, is perhaps brought home by the following quote as adequately as it could be expressed. Charles Curtis, writing about 1910, had this to say:

As to the potting material, if half a dozen experts are asked for a formula each will give one differing from the rest and yet each grower may be a splendid cultivator of cypripediums (Slippers). This sort of thing puzzles a novice, but the truth of the matter is that cypripediums are not nearly so particular over their rooting material as many other kinds of orchids. The writer has received plants potted in the usual 'general mixture' of peat and chopped sphagnum, others in material similar but with fibrous loam added, others in yellow loam only and others in fibrous loam, broken leaves and sand and in every case the plants seemed to be perfectly healthy.

Charles Curtis was an eminent authority on orchids in the early years of the twentieth century.

The plants used to start a collection of Slippers are immaterial. They may be a group of expensive clones, or hardy hybrids and species, or culls from the collections of more advanced growers. The experiences will be the same, whether the plants like the conditions or not. Sometimes imaginations run riot and the primary ideas are lost almost before they are translated into action.

The real battle to overcome is impetuous buying, not only Slippers but all sorts of orchids which do not blend into similar environments. At the beginning of the book considerable space is devoted to outlining environment, so there is no need to go over it again. A new environment must be created for growing Slippers.

The most successful cultivators specialise in the genus almost to complete exclusion of other genera. This cannot altogether be written off as over-enthusiasm, or the occasional pattern common among orchid growers of forsaking one genus for another. It is a logical extension of the idea of building glass-houses to suit one genus, rather than collections of mixed orchids. In this way, the ultimate potential of the genus is brought out, and the extended flowering season of Slippers from April or earlier to November gives almost a total annual interest that is not present with so many other genera, particularly cymbidiums.

The first species Slipper recorded as brought to England and cultivated was *Paphio. venustum* (Venus' Slipper), discovered in India by a man named Wallich very early in the 1800s. It grows at about 500-600 metres elevation and is nominally a cool-growing orchid, but grows and flowers better in a warmed glass-house.

*Paphio. venustum* is a beautiful miniature flower, the foliage tessellated or marbled in light and dark green, the undersides of the leaves purple spotted on light green, with the base of the leaf red-purple. It varies considerably, the Indian writer Pradhan listing several in his book on Indian species orchids. *Paphio. venustum* cultivates easily into large clumps and it makes a beautiful specimen plant. Because of the smallness of the flower it never became one of the prominent species, but it has a claim to fame as being one of the parents of the second hybrid Slipper registered, which was *Paphio.* Crossianum in 1873. The other parent was *Paphio. insigne*.

The larger species used to create most of the hybrids originated in India and adjacent countries. The divisions of the area are man-made, but the plants are best described as Asian. Where they came from is unknown, but they have some affinity with similar plants in South America and dissimilar, but more widespread, plants, the cypripediums, of Europe, Asia and North America. All have similar flowers and rank among the oldest orchid plants in botanical tabulations.

The various members of the Asian group of paphiopedilums all hybridise fairly readily, but few tangible results have come from more than 100 years of trying inter-generic crosses with phragmipediums and cypripediums.

The apex of the inverted pyramid of hybrids is dominated by five species. Four are Indian, the other Asian. The four Indian species are *Paphio. insigne, Paphio. vollosum, Paphio. spiceranum* and *Paphio. charlesworthii*. The Asian species is *Paphio. barbatum*. These were by no means the only species used, but they were the most important. Subsequently several others were introduced, some of which were much earlier material, and others were tried and discarded. As most of them are illustrated in color, little of that feature is described.

*Paphio. insigne* is considered the beginner's orchid. It did not get that reputation for nothing; it was earned, because it has always been the most numerous species in cultivation and has withstood years of abuse and remained alive, even if, at times, it was too weak to produce flowers. Some plants of *Paphio. insigne* which appear from time to time at meetings of orchid societies bear adequate testimony to this. They mostly appear abject looking and neglected, the leaves trailing limply over the edges of the pots, instead of upright and glossy.

*Paphio. insigne* was also discovered by Wallich in Sylhet province in north-eastern India and was first flowered in England at the Liverpool Botanic Gardens in 1820. It was also found in other parts of north-eastern India with many variations. It is a most interesting species because of these variations, but the greater part of the list of these varieties cultivated are names only because they have been lost, or should we say submerged, in the oceans of discarded orchids of other years. Several of the common varieties of the species survive, one of which is known variously as Sylhetense, and other epithets or varietal names, few of which are accurate.

Helen Adams, a well known American orchid grower, somewhere about 1954 compiled a list of the varieties of *Paphio. insigne*. It comprised ninety-six known and authenticated variations named and grown. Although few could claim enough distinction to be ranked with the varieties *sanderae* and *harefield hall,* they were considered sufficiently distinct to be given varietal names. The common form or type is illustrated.

Probably the most outstanding of all the varieties is that known as *sanderae,* which is responsible for most of the green and gold hybrids, also with something to do about the white Slippers. Another of the varieties, probably the largest, is the variety *harefield hall,* which contributed much to the size and shape of all the hybrids. It also is illustrated.

Writing in *The Orchid Review* (England) in 1916, a correspondent records: 'I saw a magnificent sight 10 days ago. One longish house with 250 pots of *Cypripedium* (*Paphiopedilum*) *insigne* variety *sanderanum,* best robust type, all in bloom on one side of the house — in one case with two flowers on a stem — and nearly the same number of *C. insigne* variety *harefield hall* opposite. They are grown nearly as cool as odontoglossums.' It is almost possible to close one's eyes and see that, if memory is worth anything.

*Paphio. insigne,* according to Pradhan, occurs now only in the state of Meghalaya, at an elevation of 1000 to 1500 metres, growing in association with scrubby vegetation on dolomite rock faces in the vicinity of watercourses. All the rest are gone.

At one time in Melbourne, George Leverett had thousands of plants of *Paphio. insigne* in glass-houses, cultivated for their flowers and later as bulk supply plants for the predecessors of the supermarkets. Most of that stock is now gone. A New Zealand grower also had a very large collection of *Paphio. insigne.*

Growing as it does at such an elevation, *Paphio. insigne* would be expected to be a cool-growing orchid. However, like so many of the genus, it grows much better with some assistance in the colder months of the year when the temperature falls below 12 degrees. A specimen plant with twelve or more flowers is still an eye-catching sight.

*Paphio. insigne* var. *sanderae* came to Sanders, England, with a batch of plants imported from India and first attracted Frederick Sanders' attention because of its foliage and the color of the stem, which was pale green instead of brown. Almost immediately a mutation or a new Slipper was forecast, and although we could not call the variety an albino, it is the yellow or lutine form of that aberration. The value placed on mutations at that time is incredible and *Paphio. insigne* var. *sanderae* was no exception, although all ranges of price have been given for initial sales, according to which author writes the story. However, it was fairly common to pay as much as 300 guineas for a single growth of this orchid when it was a rarity in collections. Translated into the currency of the 1970-80 period, it would amount to somewhere near $7500 at the most optimistic conversion factor.

*Paphio. insigne* var. *sanderae* was not an isolated mutation and several others were introduced later. One variety known as *royalty* was fairly common in Australia at one time, and the distinction between the two was so slight that the borderline has become blurred and one is now grown as the other.

Irrespective of the value and beauty of the rest of the collection, every grower of the genus should have at least one plant of the common form of *Paphio. insigne* var. *sylhetense* included with his or her orchids. If plants of other varieties can be traced and bought, these also should have a place.

*Paphio. exul* is closely related to *Paphio. insigne* in color and shape but had little to do with production of the hybrids. It is a hardy and easily flowered species which likes warm conditions, grows well into a specimen plant, and flowers in September in Australia.

It may be thought a disproportionate amount of space has been given to *Paphio. insigne,* but it is probably the most important of the species.

The variety *Paphio. insigne* var. *harefield hall* is in reality a sub-variety of *Paphio. insigne* var. *giganteum,* the habitat of which was completely stripped late in the last century. Practically nothing is known about its habitat because, even as far back as the beginning of the century, no one was sure where it came from. It was originally known as *Cypripedium insigne* var. *montanum* and was thought to have come from the Khasia Hills area of Burma.

*Paphio. villosum* is closely allied to *Paphio. insigne* in the later tables of plant relationship, although the two are so dissimilar. Like *Paphio. insigne,* it also does better when grown in a winter minimum temperature of about 12 degrees. It is far more vigorous in habit than *Paphio. insigne,* with longer and broader leaves and the ability to grow quickly into large plants with vigorous root systems. Although *Paphio. villosum* is known to grow on rock faces, in earlier literature it was mentioned as being epiphytic as frequently as lithophytic. Like *Paphio. insigne, Paphio. villosum* is scarce in areas where once there were large colonies of these Slippers, and some places have been totally denuded.

I prefer to bracket *Paphio. boxallii* with *Paphio. villosum* as two varieties rather than the separate species status usually given. While *Paphio. villosum* flowers in April to June, however, *Paphio. boxallii,* as it is known, flowers much later in the year. The stem of this orchid is much more hirsute than that of *Paphio. villosum* and as it is referred to in *Sanders Hybrid List* as a separate species, it is difficult to overcome that handicap and convert it to a varietal form.

The type form of *Paphio. villosum,* with its large, glossy brown, red-brown and gold flowers, is splendid when grown into a specimen plant. It was sent to England somewhere about 1853 by Thomas Lobb to Veitchs' nursery, where it was used with *Paphio. barbatum* to produce the hybrid *Paphio.* Harrisianum. It is an excellent plant to use as a seed-raising pot because of its profuse root system. It is uncommon to raise paphiopedilum seed this way, but quite good results can be obtained by amateur seed-raisers who do not want the expense of a lot of equipment. Perhaps the end result is a survival of the fittest; but, after all, that is nature's way of doing things.

*Paphio. villosum* originally grew in several areas in upper Burma, occasionally in dense masses high up on large trees, growing in accumulations of decaying vegetation and moss, and seldom occurring below about 1370-1525 metres (4500-5000 feet). A smaller, less colorful variety is occasionally seen, the stems much more hairy than the type form, and it was found originally in Indo-China, as it was then known.

Assam, northern India, is an area famous for species orchids of many kinds. It is the habitat — perhaps we should hope it still is and will be for ages to come — of *Paphio. spiceranum,* which was first brought to England about 1878. It flowered there about a year or so later and attracted great attention. As there were so few plants in the importation, the price quoted for divisions was quite high even for a period when novelties of any sort were expensive. It is illustrated among the photographs. Soon afterwards collectors traced the source of the first plants and a flood followed, until again the whole area was almost denuded.

A short quote from Volume 3 of *The Orchid Album* is interesting: 'It (*spiceranum*) grows on almost perpendicular cliffs and rocks, from which the plants are loosened with sticks and so let down during the months of May and September. The water hangs around the plants to keep the soil and moss which is about them as wet as the water itself. During the winter months this cypripedium should not be grown hot.'

In the years following these importations, the plants must have been killed in thousands, for at the time hybrid paphiopedilums became popular the species and early primary hybrids were discarded in huge numbers. The wealthier of the growers, too, culled their collections of species heavily, keeping only the best varieties and destroying hundreds of plants which produced poor flowers. They did not realise at the time that the gene pool of these apparently inferior types was just as important as that of the better looking species.

Much smaller occasionally than *Paphio. insigne* or *Paphio. villosum,* this new species contributed a share of characteristics to posterity, not least of which was the lovely dorsal sepal and petal median lines of rose-purple, quite obvious in many hybrids far removed from the species.

Unlike cymbidiums, where the whole emphasis of the flower is centred on the labellum, the centre of interest in a paphiopedilum flower is the dorsal or upper sepal. The labellum or pouch fails to get any attention until the authorities who judge these flowers praise or criticise it for its part in balancing the flower. Even in this it is more the shape than the color which is considered.

The labellum of *Paphio. spiceranum* is most attractively colored pale to olive green, with reticulations of purple and overtones of other color at times. The staminode, the central part of a Slipper flower, on *Paphio. spiceranum* is unusually colored.

*Paphio. charlesworthii* was one of the last Slippers to be found and brought into cultivation. Charlesworth, Shuttleworth and Co., England, presented a plant for the inspection and gratification of the Royal Horticultural Society in 1893 and it caused a sensation. It was given an Award of Merit. It was discovered in north-eastern Burma by R. Moore, a government official in the area, growing only on rocky escarpments of limestone, facing to the north or north-west. Like most orchids, it has evolved in time to a situation in which it grew best. A quote from *The Orchid Review* (England) of 1895 is interesting:

*Cypripedium charlesworthii* was discovered by me (R. Moore) at a place some 25 miles south-west of Lake Inle, the Shan States, high up on a limestone hill, fully 5000 feet above sea level. Very recently it has been gathered in quite an opposite direction, 40 miles north-east of the lake or some 60 miles from the place where it was originally found. It appears to make its home on hills of a certain formation only. In a break in a range of hills there are isolated peaks, high and precipitous, inaccessible to Europeans, and it is here that it grows. I have been out with Shans and on arriving at a particular place they, by looking at a hill, can tell you whether *C. charlesworthii* will be found there. If it occurs it will be found in large quantities and not a plant will be found on neighbouring hills of different shapes or formations. It grows fairly high up on the west and north-west slopes only, never near the base or to the east, south or south-west. The roots cling to the rocks with extraordinary tenacity, and the bigger plants could be gathered only by cutting through the roots with a 'dah' or Burmese knife. As a rule there is plenty of undergrowth around, but I have seen plants growing in the crevices of the bare rock. It grows at a higher elevation than *C. bellatulum,* but on one occasion I think I saw them growing together.

The places where *C. charlesworthii* grow are, as a rule, far removed from villages; indeed, the whole country is very sparsely populated. It is the home of the tiger, the bear, wild boar, leopard and huge snakes, and in consequence the collecting of the plant is attended with a good deal of danger. The Shans will only go out in parties of about ten and they take with them gongs which are beaten to scare away the wild beasts. When I first collected it in quantity I had thousands of flowers and I did not know then it was a new orchid.

What with tigers, bears and snakes, life certainly wasn't meant to be easy for orchid collectors, and historically most of them died an untimely death.

*Paphio. charlesworthii* is a most variable species in shape and color. The dorsal sepal is the most outstanding part and its color varies from palest pink to deep red, almost black-red. Usually the best and roundest of the dorsals are pale and a good feature is that the dorsal mostly retains its rounded shape without the reflexing which is a pronounced feature with most other species Slippers.

The recommendation that glass-houses for growing Slippers face a certain way is a simple extension of the peculiarity of *Paphio. charlesworthii* relative to its habitat, and this factor frequently accounts for the differences in cultivation of the genus from one grower to another. Convert the northern hemisphere orientation of *Paphio. charlesworthii* to a southern hemisphere equivalent and we come to a south-east to south aspect. In Australian habitats that is actually the aspect in which the greatest aggregations of most epiphytic orchids are found. But again we have been side-tracked.

When the species Slippers were numerous in their habitats *Paphio. charlesworthii* and *Paphio. spiceranum* were frequently found growing together and several supposed natural hybrids were identified in the importations which arrived in England. Many parcels of plants of *Paphio. charlesworthii* which arrived in Australia from

India for various growers in the years before quarantine and other restrictions usually comprised a matted mass of plants up to 60-90 centimetres square and in this state they were not too easy to grow. Most cultivators of this species found it difficult, but perhaps they have become more sophisticated and in the 1970-80 decade it seems more amenable, or perhaps it is better treated now it has become so rare and expensive.

*Paphio. barbatum,* from the Malaysian peninsula, is the only one of the five main species responsible for most hybrids which has tessellated or mottled foliage. This type of foliage is usually taken to indicate a need for slightly warmer cultivation. While not an infallible guide, it is one which may be safely followed. The difference would be only a matter of two or three degrees, but even this small amount is capable of increasing plant size and health.

According to collectors and observers, *Paphio. barbatum* in its habitat is left dry in a fairly long rainless period each year. It grows, however, mostly in shady valleys,

*Paphio. glanduliferum,* also illustrated in color section.

143

the roots getting sustenance from masses of detritus lodged in crevices of rocky gullies. It was a rather early addition to collections in England and Europe following its discovery about 1840.

Unlike the other four interesting species, *Paphio. barbatum* flowers much later in the year in Australia. While the four are variable, generally their period is from the beginning of May or thereabouts to September, but *barbatum* flowers as late as November. Something of this variability is obvious in the prolonged flowering period of the hybrids generally, although most of them finish as soon as the warmer months of the year push them into growth. However, it is not unusual to see flower buds in hybrids as early as February in the southern hemisphere, while the first of the species to flower, either *Paphio. insigne* or *Paphio. charlesworthii,* seldom appears before April to May.

Since the early definitions, the habitat of these various species has been extended and they are found to have a widespread but still numerically limited occurrence. It is only by maintaining the numbers that the species will be able to survive, and to this end conservation measures proposed by some countries should be adequate if properly followed by plant collectors and governments alike. It is indeed a far cry to the day when the director of the Singapore Botanic Gardens wrote in 1902: 'This well-known species is often most abundant, sometimes covering rocks in masses, as on Penang Hill. On Mount Ophir and Kedah Peak, though plentiful, it is more scattered, growing in moss by the stream in exposed places.' It is to be wondered just how many plants of *Paphio. barbatum* remain in any of those localities.

*Paphio. bellatulum* has the distinction of giving character to almost every part of the 1970-80 decade hybrid, except the ventral sepal. Originating in many parts of Asia, it grows mostly in limestone country. The leaves are among the most beautiful of the genus; not large, but fairly broad and on a well-grown plant having a crystalline lustre and depth uncommon in other orchids.

A pure white form is known, but is so rare that it is seldom seen and is possibly unknown in Australia. With *Paphio. niveum* it was responsible for the white hybrid *Paphio.* F.C. Puddle, progenitor of most of the white group.

*Paphio. niveum* is a localised species from several of the islands grouped about Malaya and Borneo and is one of the few Slippers which at times grows almost on the seashore.

*Paphio. ang thong* is also a native of islands off the same area and is frequently the subject of disagreement as to status. It is held by some to be a species in its own right, by others a natural hybrid between *Paphio. bellatulum* and *Paphio. niveum,* and by others again as a variety of *Paphio. niveum.* Some of the clones are pure white and, like *Paphio. niveum,* they have long stems.

*Paphio. delenatii* is a pink member of the same group, all of which have a similar appearance, with delicate shape and coloring, the labellum delicately egg-shaped, the petals and dorsal sepals broad, if somewhat squat. *Paphio. delenatii* has been cultivated since about 1913, when it was brought from North Vietnam to Europe by the Frenchman, Delenat. It is outstanding as probably the only paphiopedilum species to be awarded the George Moore Medal, an annual distinction for the best paphiopedilum presented to the RHS Orchid Committee, which it gained in 1931. This was an outstanding achievement, because it occurred in one of the peak periods in the hybrid development of the genus, which saw possibly the ultimate in development of the shape of things to come.

*Paphio. delenatii* was used extensively by the French hybridists Vacherot and Lecouffle, but the best of it is possibly yet to come even in this late period of its history.

The last two of this group, *Paphio. godefroyae* and *Paphio. concolor,* are similarly shaped flowers, the former with heavier markings and *Paphio. concolor* spotted all over a cream base color with tiny purple dots. Both have similar tessellated foliage which, however, does not reach the size of that of *Paphio. bellatulum.*

Of the group *Paphio. bellatulum* has the shortest stem, which is one of the disadvantages to be bred out. It is apparent in one of the outstanding clones of red Slippers of all time, *Paphio.* Paeony 'Regency', which is twice removed from *Paphio. bellatulum* in a breeding table.

*Paphio. godefroyae* was named after the wife of Monsieur Godefroy-Leboeuf, a French grower, who introduced this species somewhere about 1870. It occurs in widely separated areas of Asia and was first flowered in Kew Gardens, England. One of the first successful cultivators was Baron de Rothschild, who had a large collection of this species, as well as an extensive collection of other orchids. The family had a close association with orchids from the earliest days of their cultivation, later extending well into the 1900s.

In all, some twenty to thirty species paphiopedilums were used at various times to produce the hybrids of the last 120 years. Some were used successfully, some not persisted with after the first or second generations.

A very beautiful section came from the *Paphio. callosum* line, originating in Asia, and the *Paphio. lawrenceae* normal and albino forms. Both *Paphio. callosum* and *Paphio. lawrenceae* albinos were pale colored, striped in green on the dorsal sepal, and from them was bred a line commencing with *Paphio.* Maudiae in 1900.

In all, there are between seventy-five and eighty species paphiopedilums, but the majority, except for cultivation for their own value as beautiful species, do not have much bearing on the vast number of hybrids grown. It has been common to raise what could be called 'novelties' from the time the genus was discovered but, except for the interest of the hybridiser and an occasional fancier, in the general group of growers they have had little following.

Slippers with minority influences also have a place in the list of species and, for this reason, *Paphio. fairrieanum* ranks as a contributor. A native of Sikkim and other small areas of India, it has possibly one of the most attractive dorsal sepals of the species, as the illustration shows. It is usually found at about 1500-2000 metres, in cool country.

While this Slipper contributed color to the hybrids, the petals were a breeding handicap. Referring again to *The Orchid Album,* Volume 2, it was first cultivated and flowered by A. Fairrie, of Liverpool, England, and was named by Dr Lindley in his honor. It is appropriate to note the 'rr' in the name, as in much contemporary literature it seems to have been converted to a single consonant. In those times referred to the plant was found difficult to grow, and many better growers were of the same opinion as that held so many years later, that the chief fault was the tendency to divide the plants into single growths or small portions, a habit resented by most members of the genus.

*Paphio. hirsutissimum* is one of the species which never gained much ground in orchid collections throughout its history. It was originally sent to England in 1857 by a collector named Simons from Assam, where so many of the other species originated, and first flowered for a nurseryman named Parker.

A sister of Mr Fairrie, after whom the species *fairrieanum* was named, exhibited a painting of *hirsutissimum* somewhere about 1855, so the plants sent by Simons to England must have been the second consignment, unless she also used a drawing or a painting as her model.

John Day, another famous painter of orchid pictures, in 1885 made the following note following his portrayal of the flower: 'When the flower first expands the remarkable undulations of the edges of the petals are not apparent, but they develop in two or three days. No doubt the edges keep growing longer than the central part and therefore must undulate.' Probably this is still not verified, as the species has not a lot of admirers.

*Paphio. callosum* was originally collected from what was known as Annam, a part of Indo-China divided into several small national portions in the wake of the early history of that country, and still in process of sorting out in the late twentieth century.

It has sufficient merit in its own right to take a proud place in any collection but proves a difficult species to cultivate. It always seems to stunt the root system and possibly this is the fault of growing mediums as much as any other cause. One of the finest collections of this species ever grown in Australia was in the glass-houses of Alex Burns, an entomologist, at Blackburn, Victoria, about the 1930 period. It was growing mostly in a mixture of fibre and moss and I always found that a most satisfactory medium for the plant or two I grew. It was first brought into cultivation about 1885 after a considerable time given to a search for its habitat.

In the year 1900 Edward Low, England, imported a consignment of plants from Annam: 'We have been fortunate enough to bloom two quite novel and distinct 'albino' forms from amongst our large importation of *Cypripedium callosum* received last summer, something like 16000. The first is after *Cypripedium callosum sanderae* except that the ground color is decidedly yellow rather than the clear green of the earlier named variety, and the extremities of each petal are just tinged with purple. This plant we called *Cypripedium callosum aureum*. . .' Not so much the distinction of having found an albino form of *Paphio. callosum* is noteworthy, as the fact that they imported 16000 plants. Where, oh where, are they now!

The secret of growing this beautiful species seems to lie in cultivating it in what would be so small a pot as to appear ridiculous for any other orchid. In cultivation the almost green and white leaves are usually much smaller than those of jungle-grown plants, and the root system always seems to be sparse and short, with the new growths slow to make root even in their second year. As a cultivated species it needs studying, but the long-stemmed purple and green flowers repay all the attention.

*Paphio. victoria-regina* (synonym *Paphio. victoria-mariae*) as a species is a group embracing several of the species similar to *Paphio. chamberlainianum,* once known by their varietal names as separate species. There is little doubt that this submission is the correct one, as the members are all found in the islands of Indonesia and are too obviously variants of one theme to be given separate listing.

*Paphio. chamberlainianum* was named in honor of Joseph Chamberlain, a noted orchid grower of the last century. It was introduced from Sumatra by Sanders in 1892 and one of the earliest observations on this Slipper was the note that one of the flower stems had thirty-two bracts, indicating that it had flowered over a considerable period. Although it is not naturally inclined to produce this number in cultivation, it has been recorded as having produced twenty-seven flowers.

*Paphio. glaucophyllum* was introduced into English collections about the year 1900 and, although the foliage of this Slipper is different from that of *chamberlainianum,* the flowers are remarkably similar except in color. There are other members of the group divided solely on the score of color, notable among them *Paphio. primulinum,* which was discovered, lost, and again discovered all in the space of some sixty years. This form of *Paphio. victoria-regina* is a lovely green color.

As a group these Slippers must be fairly old in the time scale of evolution, as each of the sub-species has reached an established form which persists with little variation in their various habitats. As additions to orchid collections, they offer long-flowering seasons and fairly long-lasting flowers.

Most of the other Slippers illustrated in the color pages are not relevant to hybridising in the way that the main group is, and information on them can be found in other literature. They are nice additions to orchid collections, providing flowers when other Slippers do not, and at times exciting the envy of other growers. Although most of them are difficult to buy locally, they can nearly always be located in lists of seed-raisers and are well worth the trouble of either quarantine, if imported, or perhaps the rather high price asked for sometimes tiny seedling plantlets.

# Phragmipediums

Most of the second branch of the Slipper family, the phragmipediums, come from the west coast countries of South America, Venezuela, Colombia, Ecuador and Peru. They are seldom seen in cultivation and this is regrettable, because they are just as attractive as the paphiopedilums. Taken in as part of a Slipper collection, they can be treated in exactly the same way as paphiopedilums, suffer the same diseases and pests and have similar, though perhaps a little finer, root systems than most of the hybrid Slippers.

Perhaps the most remarkable of these orchids are those in which the petals reach lengths of up to 40 centimetres (about 15-18 inches). There are three or more such species and, like their counterparts in the paphiopedilums, it is a never-ending source of surprise that this length of petal could eventuate from so small a bud. Watching the buds open and develop is a fascinating sight because in some of the species the petals are folded once or more, first open to their full length and then grow over a period of some days to their final dimensions.

The habitats of the phragmipediums are most varied; from epiphytic perches high in the trees of the heavy rainforest areas, to places where, on the edges of rivers and in rock crevices, they are at times completely covered by floodwaters. Most of them, despite these original environments, fit quite well into glass-house culture.

Some have many flowers on long spikes similar to *Phrag. lindleyanum,* on which they grow to a metre or more with ten or more flowers. Mostly the flowers of the species are pink to dull red, and green or light yellow-green, but the species *Phrag. schlimii* varies from white to pink, as in the color illustration.

Like the paphiopedilums, the species are comparatively pest and disease free in good cultivation. But where the paphiopedilums have evolved into some seventy-five or more species, the phragmipediums have only about a dozen members of their group.

Cypripediums
This third branch of the family, which may at one time have been the first and only branch, has little to do with this story about orchid cultivation, because they are seldom so cultivated. They are purely terrestrial and, like all the other terrestrial orchids of the earth, are slowly disappearing as humans occupy more of the land once given over to natural flora.

# The work of the Hybridists

Slippers were among the earliest orchids hybridised and a long period has been devoted to them. The first was discovered and brought into cultivation in England somewhere about 1816. Some of the large homes in Australia had a glass-house, or conservatory as it was known, with collections of Slippers about the year 1900, so that they have also been cultivated here for a long time. The character of collections of these orchids has changed considerably since then, and it could be said of the 1970-80 plants that they are more a product of their environment than most other orchids.

The combination of the original species into unrecognisable hybrid forms has intensified over more than 100 years of cross-pollinating and returns have been made occasionally to various species to stiffen up and reintroduce new genes to the pool. It would be wrong to say that the old bloodlines got tired, as it seemed the further they were extended, the more robust the plants and flowers became. Over the years since the beginning of hybridising, the number registered with *Sanders List of Orchid Hybrids* runs to about 13 000 and during the 1970-80 decade a boom took place, with Slippers in demand throughout the world.

*Paphio*. Harrisianum, the first registered hybrid named, came from two early importations, *Paphio. barbatum* and *Paphio. villosum,* the cross-pollination being made by James Dominy. Although other hybridists also made this cross and named it, it was finally named after the man in whose collection it first flowered, somewhere about 1869. Subsequently, superior clones were selected and later used in secondary hybrids.

From so small a beginning has grown the enormous and complex family of the new generations in the late 1900s. It did not all grow from *Paphio* Harrisianum. As a matter of fact, the largest branches of the tree grew from the amalgamation of *Paphio. insigne* and paphiopedilums *spiceranum* and *villosum*. All this can be found by referring to Sander's list, and we are fortunate that Frederick Sander took the trouble to find out which name had precedence.

Veitch and Sons' hybridist, J. Seden, also did considerable work with the genus and quite a lot of work in the associated group of phragmipediums, or selenipediums as they were known. At that time, they were also grouped with the true terrestrial cypripediums, but most of the inter-generic work failed and, except for one or two isolated cross-pollinations, they are still intractable.

*Paphio. insigne* could perhaps be called the kingpin because it brought two significant breeding varieties into the hybridists' hands. While many forms have been given varietal names, *Paphio. insigne* var. *sanderae* and *Paphio. insigne* var. *harefield hall* were the most prominent.

While *Paphio. insigne* var. *sanderae* is frequently termed an albino, the epithet is incorrect because the flower is predominantly gold and yellow, with little white apart from the tip of the dorsal.

If precedence is considered, it is probable various people would see the species in a different order. *Paphio. spiceranum* played a part in bringing a rounded dorsal, or what is usually regarded as the main part of the flower. Although it reflexes in the species, hybridists succeeded in flattening it out while retaining the rounded outline they sought.

Others would see the outstanding dorsal of *Paphio. charlesworthii* as a predominant feature in later hybrids. Mostly it is for individuals to sort it all out and have a preference, as there is a lot to be said of the petals of *Paphio. villosum,* the median dividing lines of which are so obvious a feature of most hybrid flowers. The same species contributed a little broadness to the petals, because if hybridists had relied on the petals of *Paphio. charlesworthii* they would have been pinning their faith on the worst feature of the flower. All the good features were looked at and the task of embodying them all in the one flower still haunts hybridists. The number of hybrids raised, flowered, and finally discarded exceeds the named and valued clones by some hundreds to one, possibly a proportion common to orchids generally. How to overcome this disproportionate ratio, at times seeming within reach, has been time-consuming. White cattleyas were successfully taken to this stage, but few other genera could claim the distinction.

With paphiopedilums we get back to the theory or possibility of creating new genes to project a different shape, color or habit into hybrid Slippers. The fundamental question of whether this is possible is one I cannot answer but, with the limited knowledge I have, it appears to me that the genes are possibly there all the time as recessives waiting for the right combination to bring them forward. It is not nature's system at all, because the preference there is for breeding stability of a common line. The aim of hybridists is exactly opposite; they want all the recessives, with the inherent weaknesses thrown in.

Most Slipper growers know what the characteristics are and buy plants, mostly seedlings, keeping the outstanding clones and discarding the rest. These discards are

Slipper breeding is aimed at a rounded outline and this view of a flower is one all judges will take when assessing its shape.

the correct material for beginning a collection. They are not so important that mistakes cannot be made with them, and when done with the experimental material can be sold off again.

The recognisable characteristics inherited from the various species in Slipper hybrids are rather hard to indicate unless close examinations of the flowers are made. Individual growers, if asked to define any of these characteristics, would frequently falter, despite the fact that each of them would have a preference for a certain type of flower. Although the only guides in selecting seedlings are the parents used, they have a habit of bringing out very undesirable features and are full of deception.

In general, the species have produced three main lines — the solid colored forms, either red, green or white, or combinations of those colors, and brown; the spotted dorsal types, regardless of the base color or the color of the spots; and the striped flowers from the *Paphio. callosum* line and its albinos. Mostly it is the dorsal that is the recognition point, not the petals. Ventral sepals are mostly pale green and play little part in the quality of the flower, other than framing the labellum or pouch. Some codes for judging this part of the flower place penalties for inclusion of color in the ventral sepal, despite the fact that the hybridist intends to breed in this feature.

The ultimate aim of the hybridist is to produce a flower with a fairly flat profile in which the dorsal sepal retains a circular shape without reflexing behind the petals. The outline or overall shape is also intended to be as circular as possible. However, the system of judging flowers is rather transient and unco-ordinated, with each country imposing a different set of guidelines, mostly adjusted periodically to suit standards imposed by fanciers.

The red tones are inherited from two sources, *Paphio. barbatum* and *Paphio. charlesworthii*; the greens, golds and yellows, and whites from the species *paphiopedilums spiceranum, insigne* var. *sanderae* and both *bellatulum* and *niveum*. Most of the spotting is attributable to *Paphio. insigne* var. *harefield hall,* while *Paphio. villosum* and *Paphio. boxallii* blend in with the red-browns. Some influence may also be supposed for *Paphio. barbatum* in the spotted types.

It is hard to put an exact date to the appearance of Slippers which had outstanding influence on future generations, because it was a continuity from both *Paphio.* Harrisianum in 1869 and *Paphio.* Leeanum in 1884, as well as a number of other registered hybrids in Frederick Sander's first list.

Among the early surprises in hybridising were a number of Slippers which so closely resembled the flowers which showed up in importations of species. *Paphio.* Leeanum was one of these and it indicated quite clearly that the cross-pollination of the species in their habitat was not only to be expected, but had actually occurred. There were a number of others, too.

Anyone interested enough to go through the hybrid list and tabulate the pedigrees of the red-tinted section will almost certainly find a basic entry to the credit of *Paphio.* Harrisianum. The cross-pollination of this hybrid and *Paphio. charlesworthii* produced *Paphio.* Bingleyense, which, in the chaotic sort-out of all the personal records of the various hybridists, was also known as *Paphio.* Redstart. The name is significant enough without explanations and this Slipper is also among the illustrations. It was also known as a Bingleyense hybrid and is one of the unfortunate casualties in the paphiopedilum hybrid list for which no true antecedents are known. Sander's hybrid list indicates it as the last-named — a distinct Bingleyense hybrid.

Although perhaps *Sander's List of Orchid Hybrids* certainly has the last say, *Paphio.* Redstart 'Exbury' appeared in an exhibit in 1932 from Lionel de Rothschild before the Royal Horticultural Society with parentage appended — *Paphio.* Nubian x *Paphio.* Mrs Cary Batten. So perhaps that is where it all rests, in another of the mysteries of hybridising following indiscriminate cross-pollinations and poor book-keeping. Yet the most ironic twist to that story is the fact that neither of the two parents cited by Lionel de Rothschild had known antecedents, either. So just how much did he know about the real breeding?

This, of course, means that it has some *Paphio. villosum* in its background and it led finally to the presentation in 1957 of *Paphio*. Paeony 'Regency' to the Orchid Committee of the RHS, a red hybrid that changed the shape of things to come. It was given an Award of Merit.

There were so many outstanding primary and secondary hybrids that it is impossible to select a clone and say that it was pre-eminent. So many contributed something to the general line that, while several can be noted as having contributed certain characteristics such as size or color, others will need to be added to the list because of their contributions, however small they were. If a final choice was forced, the primary hybrid *Paphio* Leeanum would probably have to be given the vote, because it contributed several forms or clones bred from the *Paphio. insigne* varieties *harefield hall* and *sanderae*. Its partner in both instances was *Paphio. spiceranum*. An outstanding form of *Paphio*. Leeanum was raised by G. F. Moore in 1914, and this had a far greater impact than any other previous variety.

As with these orchids, it is also difficult to pick out any person above others as the greatest contributor to the future of the genus, but probably G. F. Moore and his grower, W. H. Page, would be equal to any of them, including F. C. Puddle, whose speciality was white Slippers.

One of the confusing factors is inclusion in the hybrid list of *Paphio. villosum* and *Paphio. boxallii* as separate species. There is a great amount of this orchid in the spotted section as well as the red section. The dorsal of *Paphio. boxallii* is variable, with solid color and blotches of light to dark red-brown. The primary hybrid from this orchid and *Paphio. spiceranum* is *Paphio*. Calypso. It should be synonymous with *Paphio*. Lathamianum if the relationship between the two is considered varietal. There is little doubt that both the spotted and the red sections of the hybrids are indebted to *Paphio. boxallii*.

In the twelfth generation *Paphio*. Copperware, with almost orange tones in the dorsal sepal of some clones, there are at least six infusions of *Paphio. boxallii* in the pedigree.

The spotted section must have come from *Paphio. insigne,* with the variety *harefield hall* probably having a greater effect than smaller varieties. We are looking at the wrong end of the breeding table to know what really went on when various hybridists introduced better forms of primary and secondary hybrids. In effect, we can only look at the blank spaces and suppositions in the first stages of the hybrid list and finally settle on second and third generation hybrids for allocating precedence or fame.

Several Slippers come to the forefront, among which was *Paphio*. Cardinal Mercier, supposed to have come from *Paphio*. Lathamianum, which is the result of cross-pollinating *Paphio. villosum* and *Paphio. spiceranum*. The hybrid list further confuses us by stating a belief that there must have been other influences to produce such a flower. It was a very good red, but also produced some first class spotted flowers.

Paphiopedilums Christopher, Hera, Alcibiades, Actaeus and the *Paphio*. Nitens complex also played a part in the spotted group, as well as the clear colored Slippers. The elaboration of the beautiful spotting of the dorsal is still going on, despite the thought in the 1930 peak of the evolution of the hybrids that the epitome had been reached in *Paphio*. Cameo, a Slipper never destined to fulfil the great expectations for it at the time. Others seem to have taken all the honors.

When it comes down to absolute size, few hybrids reached the proportions of *Paphio*. Grand Monarch, at least one clone of which had a magnificent dorsal sepal about 13 centimetres (5 inches) across. It would appear that there was only one clone of this hybrid and it was never registered in that name.

Discussion on the merits of the hybrids and their inherent qualities could be endless, because there are now some 13000 registered. Some critical gaps occur where breeding is unknown, and there is little knowledge of the varieties used.

Occasionally hybridists were either too busy or too careless and failed to register their work with the RHS. This still happens and causes endless complications with other genera as well as paphiopedilums, as unnamed crosses are used in further hybridising.

*Paphio*. Grand Monarch was owned by a New South Wales grower named Walter Fahey and it gained for him a First Class Certificate and silver medal from the Orchid Society of New South Wales in 1946. It proved a most difficult orchid to grow and later the plant died out. It was believed to have been imported originally by a Victorian grower from England somewhere about the early 1930 period, the parentage unknown.

While several species contributed to the production of the various self-colors like the green and yellow Slippers, the primary hybrid *Paphio*. Leeanum is most prominent, particularly the forms emerging from use of *Paphio. insigne* var. *sanderae* and *Paphio. insigne* var. *harefield hall*. The amalgamation of this line with the *Paphio. bellatulum* group brought forward secondary hybrids which have an effect up to the tenth generation and beyond.

*Paphio*. Actaeus was the result of back-crossing *Paphio*. Leeanum with the two better varieties of *Paphio. insigne,* so a certain amount of inbreeding is common to almost the total line of hybrids which followed the production of such Slippers as *Paphio*. Hera (*Paphio. boxallii* x *Paphio*. Leeanum), *Paphio*. Christopher (*Paphio*. Actaeus x *Paphio*. Leeanum) and *Paphio*. Monsieur de Curte (*Paphio. boxallii* x *Paphio. insigne*), which in some considerations could also be called *Paphio*. Nitens.

The selection of the various parents to produce the clear-color hybrids was relatively easy because the so-called albino or lutine genes of *Paphio. insigne* var. *sanderae* were dominant and the follow-up simply had to concentrate on shape of the petals and dorsal, which could be taken from the *Paphio. bellatulum-niveum* line to achieve a quite shapely clear-color flower.

With the whites such as *Paphio*. F.C. Puddle, a separate grouping emerging from *Paphio. insigne* var. *sanderae,* but with the white genes dominant instead of the lutine or yellow genes, it was again a matter of concentrating on the *Paphio. bellatulum-niveum* complex and being content with a somewhat smaller flower. The primary hybrid *Paphio*. Psyche (*Paphio. bellatulum* x *Paphio. niveum*) controlled this factor for several generations.

There were other small white hybrids such as *Paphio*. Boltonii, the parentage of which was not recorded, and *Paphio*. Albion (*Paphio*. Astarte x *Paphio. niveum*), but they were diversions which never had such a future as the mainline hybrids.

Some idea of the success of the pot-sown method of raising seed is conveyed by the verified account of a sowing by Mr Hunter, orchid grower for the Earl of Tankerville, in Northumberland, England, recorded by the *Gardeners Chronicle* in 1906: 'The seed of the cross-pollination of *C*. Leeanum x *C. insigne* var. *harefield hall* was sown in May, 1905, and the first plant flowered in November, 1906, with a second plant flowering soon after.' Perhaps it was only a secondary hybrid and vigorous, but in the 1970-80 decade it is a fortunate hybridist who can flower them in under four years, let alone a period of some seventeen months.

# Pots and Potting

The root system of most hybrid Slippers is rather coarse, mostly covered in a fine, hair-like outer coat or skin. It is variable in this regard, some having quite smooth roots like cymbidiums. The root system is brittle and easily damaged.

If all the activity is centred about the top of the potting material it is obvious that something is wrong. The roots should penetrate right through to the bottom of the pot and curl around, or even emerge through the drainage holes or slits. One way to encourage this penetration is to keep the potting medium just slightly dryer than the bench for most of the time.

Apart from the foliage, the main morphological difference between the tessellated or mottled leaf species and the plain green leafed species is the root system. In the main green leafed species the systems are fairly long, extensive, branched and mostly hairy or hirsute. This is not constant, but in most hybrids it emerges as a general feature. In the tessellated leaf group, such as *Paphio. callosum* and most of the others, the system is short, bare, and at times crass, particularly in the species mentioned and the *Paphio. bellatulum* complex.

Quite aside from the type of roots developed by these species in their habitats, pot-grown plants tend to have a major inheritance of both leaves and roots when interbred and produce short roots, and few of them when compared with the systems produced by developments from the green leafed species. They should be grown in much smaller pots and additions of old mortar, or some form of slowly soluble limestone derivatives, seem to promote healthier growth and flowering. Dolomite or shell grit is far too slow and the potting material is frequently discarded in repotting before any beneficial break-down occurs.

Free lime sprinkled on the top of the potting material and watered through seems to fulfil a useful function and plants treated in this way, provided the mix is congenial in the first place, seem to get benefit from it.

Since the environment and potting materials were so well covered in the section on cymbidiums there is little point in going over it all again, except to note the modifications regarding shade and benching and possibly a slight adjustment of the potting material to cope with a little more frequent watering, damping down and humidifying.

The actual repotting and dividing is more a matter of following the illustrated section than one of explanation. Points to remember are that the plants resent division into single growths, or propagations too small and unrooted to proceed naturally into their clumps. The clump or multiplication is less a feature of hybrids beyond the first and second generation than of the primaries and species. As the size of the plants and the economics of growing them changes, they are possibly best repotted every second or third year and kept within reasonable dimensions.

One of the problems encountered here is that when the plant is repotted without division the root system is too big to go back into the same pot. If this system is not too intense a certain amount of the mix can be eased out and fresh materials worked into the pot without disturbing the root ball. This is not an ideal procedure and within reason the plant should be put into the next size of pot, or root-pruned to fit back into the old one. If culture is good, neither of these procedures will go against the plant. However, it should be done later in the year when new root tips are visible and not with the general start of repotting about the end of August.

No Slippers should be handled before the beginning of October in cool climates where there is a risk of a cold snap without adequate heating systems to keep the temperature up about the 15 degrees Celsius mark to promote root activity.

The type of pots used is open to question, some growers preferring clay pots, others quite at home with plastics. But it is best to remember, despite advice given in good faith, what suits one grower and one glass-house does not necessarily suit another. The most urgent thing to remember is not to mix them. My preference remains for clay pots for a completely honest and simple reason — the clay pot stays moist right through and this can be felt on the outside by hand as well as on the inside by the roots. However, both types have advantages.

The composition of the mix should be slightly different for plastic pots, with a little more drainage material, whether it is granulated plastic, gravel or scoria, and a little coarsening of the other material. Some of the drainage material may be replaced by shell grit but, contrary to some opinions, there is no advantage from its calcareous nature. Where it appears to be successfully integrated it could be put down more to good general culture than any benefit derived from the shell grit.

It will be found that if a mix is made up with no fertiliser whatever there is not enough natural nutriment in it to satisfy a Slipper. If the plant is examined, the leaves are quite thick and contain a lot of liquid. They need feeding and, growing naturally, get most of this nutriment from decaying leaves in the form of phosphoric acid and trace elements.

A cymbidium mix which contains no decay material to release the plant food needed by Slippers should have it added. Such mixes could consist of rice hulls, peat-moss and gravel; peanut shell, bark, peat-moss and gravel; or various combinations, which are almost sterile unless organic fertilisers are added. While there is no reason to condemn mixtures with organic fertilisers, they are not the most suitable to begin with. Perhaps with a bit of sophistication and knowledge they could be made into the best mixes possible.

Leafy decay material is one of the best natural sources of nutrient for Slippers, possibly starting with oak leaf and if it is not available most other hard deciduous leaf as second best, followed by evergreen leaves which have begun to break down. Never use green leaf. Pine needles have been used successfully, but they should be reduced to a black, crumbly stage. They may be used with tan bark, pine bark, and gravel, and they also blend well with wood chip mixes which are infrequently used for Slippers.

One of the best materials, which may be used without any additives at all, is tan bark. If it is available a plant should be given a trial run to see if it is suitable. The trial time should be in the growing season, looking for root activity. Non-active roots or browned-off tips would indicate incorrect acidity and it should be discarded, or tested to get a reading so that a corrective could be used. If it is suitable and used, the plants should preferably be repotted every year into fresh bark known to be similar. If it is unknown, a fresh test pot should be run through.

It is always a good idea to run a test plant in any mix along with the general collection to look for improvements in cultivation, but do not run more than one or two at a time. It is almost inevitable that *Paphio. insigne* will be used as the 'guinea pig' when the plants regarded as expendable should really be the poorer hybrids.

Variations through a collection should be avoided and plants brought into a collection should be repotted into the general mix as soon as possible, using the same type of pot and discarding odd plastic pots with a different pattern of drainage holes or slits. If clay pots are used the drainage pattern should be made as consistent as possible, with an enlarged hole, the same sized crocks, and the same depth of crocks. Within reason, the better a pattern is followed the more even the growth patterns and flowering will be. Keep the small pots and the larger ones grouped in their respective sizes as far as possible.

Lumps of old mortar are different material to mortar made with cement. Brick-layer's mortar is made with lime and sand and this is the type of material intended. If a

154

grower is sufficiently interested to make up a mortar and let it harden, season and mature in the weather for twelve months, then break it up and use it, there is no better addition to a Slipper mix. While the roots do not always attach to it, the plants will stay healthy and a difference can be noticed in the leaves.

Charcoal as a drainage material or non-decay additive to a Slipper mix has nothing to recommend it over scoria or gravel, except that it may be more readily obtained. Occasionally when lumps are included in a potting mix, roots will be found clinging to them when repotting, but this is because it has absorbed something they need. When using a coke-fired boiler I used the ash clinkers as a part of the drainage additive and when repotting always found roots attached to some of the lumps, while other lumps were avoided by the roots. I let them sort it out. Coke-fired boilers have gone and with them the ash, but mortar is still available if needed.

Every constituent of a Slipper mix should be included for a reason and not added on the basis that maybe it will do something. The simplest, such as plain tan bark only or a simple three-part mix of leaf, bark and gravel, are very easy to control and may also be easily fertilised.

Considering the nature of the plants, I have never believed that they could be grown in sphagnum moss with no supplementary feeding. In the many years I grew them, I could always get roots on the plants in this way if they refused to grow them any other way, but inevitably they had to be put into a fertilised mix to get the flowers. If fed in the sphagnum moss, however weak the solution, the moss always decayed first, followed by the roots. It was a tedious and boring process, too, and quite unsuitable for a collection of anything like the proportions grown by most fanciers.

Usually the basic mix without added fertiliser will be found inadequate to bring the plants into flower with ultimate stem length and flower size. Whatever additives are used should be minimal and the right type to do what is needed. They may consist of blood and bone worked into the top of the potting material, or such other quick-release fertilisers that suit the genus. I always favored blood and bone because it was what could be termed a 'natural' food. The usual application should be quite small and applied twice a year; in November, when the plant is growing, and again at the end of February, when the flowers should be forming in the growths. For a 15 centimetres (6 inches) pot a large teaspoon of blood and bone worked into the top of the potting material is quite sufficient. It should be spread evenly over the surface. A week later the same amount of free lime should be sprinkled over the surface and watered through the mix.

Pot size should be adequate for the plant concerned, but a general average over the collection should be a mixture of 12 and 15 centimetre (5½ and 6 inch) pots for hybrid Slippers in good health. Where a plant has few or no roots, it should be started off again in fresh sphagnum moss, potted into the general mix when the new roots show, and again taken out and examined about six weeks later to see how the roots are progressing. If they are not growing, the plant should be put through the system again. It does little harm to any plant to see how the root system is progressing.

While some orchids do not like to be benched closely, Slippers may be closed up tightly without ill effects. Irrespective of the benching, closed or open, they should be staged up progressively toward the rear of the bench so that all the plants are visible, the smallest at the front and up to the largest at the back, which would be in about 15-centimetre pots. Labels should be clear and firmly inserted, as there are already too many Slippers with no names, some of them wrongly named and many with illegible guesswork tags. Always print the name fully, as any abbreviations could lead to mistakes.

This is a collection of species paphiopedilums. As most of them grow only small plants they will never graduate to large pots, so they should be grouped like these Slippers on a tray of mixed old bark, shell grit, charcoal and other filling. Unlike the large pots, there is no reserve of moisture and if such small plants are grown on open benches with normal sized hybrids they will dry out much sooner and perhaps become dehydrated. Small propagations with little root also appreciate this treatment.

For small propagations, of whatever genus, there is no treatment more conducive to getting them into growth than a small 'hot-box'. This one is electrically heated through low-voltage sub-surface wire units which keep the moisture-retaining filling at about 22 degrees Celsius (72 degrees Fahrenheit). The little dial-type thermometer pictured is a pre-Celsius model. Small Slipper seedlings if slow to get away also react vigorously in this type of humidicrib. However, there are always some which are naturally weak and even the hot-box sometimes fails to get a response.

156

Some paphiopedilums are slow to propagate, particularly tessellated foliage types, and they should be encouraged to make growth from the older flowered sections of the plants, which slowly fade away unless something is done to spur them into growth. This type of propagation, however, should also be adopted with any Slippers which are slow to show a multiplying tendency. In this picture the plant is forced into sections with the thumbs, grasping each section firmly, but only partially severing the rhizome for preference, then tying the two sections together again to hold them firm. It is possible for one section to have little root, but the partially severed rhizome will force that section to make new roots. This system is best done at maximum growth season.

A sharp knife may also be used to cut through the rhizome between flowered and leading portions of Slipper plants, but there is a danger of severing some roots as well. This process should always be carried out in the season before that proposed as the repotting time for the plant. By the time potting comes around it is probable that both sections will have new rooted growths and a good start. If necessary after severing the two portions of the plant, either with the thumbs or a knife, it may be wise to tie the sections together again to keep them firm in the pot until they are repotted the following season.

The potting material frequently becomes useless before the Slipper plants show signs of needing a break-up or repotting. It is always better to catch them at this stage, with new roots showing from the forward growths, which may happen at any time from August onward. Some Slippers have a bad annual cycle which shows up when the plants are removed from pots and the grower finds that neither the forward growth nor the one behind it have any roots at all. In this instance it sometimes helps the plant to move by partially severing the rhizome between the rooted portion of the plant and the unrooted portion. 'Careful' is the way to go about this, so that the severance is not made total. Again tie the two portions together so that a split cannot occur.

157

Total penetration and elaboration of the root system occurs more frequently in species Slippers like this plant of *Paphio. villosum* than in most of the modern hybrids, but the aim should always be to try for this type of root system, no matter how far removed from species the plant may be. There is little trouble in unravelling the root systems of most Slippers, but the handling should be gentle and the aim saving as much of the system as possible, even if it may need shortening to get a correct pot size enclosing it.

Always be generous in taking propagations from Slipper plants. Allow plenty of root to each division, even if it means at times an apparent sacrifice of an additional plant of a good clone. Propagations with little root take a lot longer to establish and if the divisions are too drastic it is possible to lose a propagation entirely or at least add some years to the time it may take to get another division, as the first things that go are the old flowered growths. If these leaves seem to be losing vitality and tend to turn yellowish at the tips, clip them to half their length and smear some anti-fungus powder and lime on the cut end. Usually they heal up and the part-leafed propagation will stabilise until the plant gets into growth.

It is the root system which should match the pot used, not the rest of the plant, however incongruous the leaf system may look when the job is finished. It may be necessary to repot again the following year, but if a meagre root system is put into a large pot in the hope that it will soon make up the difference, the opposite is usually the result — the potting mix sours with too little root activity and possibly some of the good root which was put into the large pot will also deteriorate.

Some Slipper growers regard crocks in the bottom of the pot as waste of space. The amount of crock in this pot is clearly visible. It amounts to about a quarter of the depth. It is far from wasted, as the roots demonstrate. Whatever nutrient is washed through the mix to the bottom of the pot finds roots waiting there to absorb it. Root penetration is frequently missed by using uncongenial potting mixes; neglecting to water thoroughly, with the consequence of a dry lower area in the mix; sometimes from overwatering, resulting in the roots rotting before they get very far into the potting compost.

Clay pots usually have more slope to the sides than plastic pots and for various reasons still have a following in orchid growing, in spite of the difficulty occasionally in getting them. If they are used the drainage hole should be enlarged in a fashion similar to this, making sure that the crock which covers the hole does not seal it. Some of the growers who use these pots take as much care with the positioning of the crocks as in making up their mix. If converting to plastic pots, all the collection should be repotted in the one year, leaving none in the clay pots to cause cultural problems. Watering is perhaps the main feature to watch after conversion, because the use of plastics will lessen its frequency.

159

# Plants and Seedlings

Slippers may be bought in only two forms: as propagations or as seedlings. Cymbidiums and many other genera are available also as meristem propagations, a system not so far successfully mastered with Slippers.

Seedlings are always a challenge as, irrespective of the genus, a batch from one cross-pollination will always have different growth rates among them, some growing fast and soon leaving the others plodding along. The growth rate is no indication whatsoever of quality or size of flowers, or even health, as some of the plodders seem to take a little longer initially but make up for the waiting.

When bought, seedlings should be put into as small a pot as they will fit — usually a 5-7 centimetre pot is adequate. These pots are much better if they are clay rather than plastic, so that they can be stood on a wet gravel bed. Such a small pot holds so little potting material that it could be either too wet or too dry without any real indication of its condition. Clay pots stood on a wet to damp gravel or shell grit bed seldom need watering, as they soak up enough moisture by capillary action to keep them in a moisture-stable condition. All the plants need is a light overhead spray occasionally through the day to keep the humidity high.

Small plants like seedlings should not be overpotted at any stage. Leave them in the small pots, no matter how incongruous they may appear, until it is obvious from sheer size or root activity that they should be put into something larger. The move should be into the same style of pot as the general collection. If plastics are used, then their move from the small clay pot will be into plastic. Occasionally the seedlings may include a few which for some reason never seem to get a root system going. These should be put into a small ball of lightly pressed growing sphagnum moss, and returned to the damp gravel bed. When they develop roots they should be put into the potting mix and given another try.

There is nearly always a death rate among the small Slipper seedlings and it is usually a natural sort-out, not related in any way to disease. The only real susceptibility they all have is to fungus. This can be held off with sprays designed for this purpose and used about once a fortnight, always in a weak solution.

Nothing much is ever said or written about nutrient sprays for Slippers but, provided the concentration is very weak, any one of several may be used. Maxicrop, a seaweed derivative, is very efficient as a fertiliser and some idea of the concentration containing sufficient for small Slippers may be gained from a color test, with enough added to turn water a very pale honey color. With fertilisers like Aquasol or similar concentrates, a teaspoonful to 18 litres of water would be an equivalent. Strong concentrations lead to root loss as surely as overwatering.

Lack of success with meristem propagating may be put on the debit side, because it would simplify the system considerably. The reasons could be obscure, but breeding or morphological instability are probably the causes.

Most Slippers are bought on sight, the same as cymbidiums but, as the seedlings are so small and manageable up to flowering size, there is incentive to buy them rather than expensive propagations and at times to buy more than can be accommodated when they grow.

Some work has been done on chromosome counting with the species and it seems that they do not run to a regular pattern as a genus at all, if the counts published are accurate. While *Paphio. insigne* seems to be fairly consistent with a chromosome count of 26, there is a variation from this figure by two or three other studies, which suggest 28 in one instance and 24 in another, and even some tetraploid forms with counts of 52. *Paphio. spiceranum* varies from 28 to 30, while other species have up to 40 as published counts.

All this is possibly reflected in the failure of some clones to set seed capsules or to mature what turn out to be empty or nearly empty capsules. So much work needs to be done on this project, having little or no commercial value, and the start is being made so late in the hybrid development that it is going to be a mammoth task to sort it all out. It may be a breakthrough for meristemming, however, if it was started. A good deal of amateur hit-or-miss hybridising and cross-pollinating results from this lack of knowledge, with visual aspects of parents too frequently outweighing a little basic research into antecedents back to primary hybrid or species level.

Outstanding clones are subject to judgment on a number of grounds, but at all times shape seems to be a paramount consideration. It is too frequently predetermined in sets of inflexible standards, with little scope for individual preference or the best features of a flower, such as color.

Most of the breeding is aimed at a market which fluctuates in fairly wide periods or waves. In the 1970-80 decade the peak of such a wave occurred, with the previous relatively high peak occurring some thirty years earlier and the preceding peak approximately the same span earlier still. Perhaps the peaks are economically activated, with that of 1970-80 certainly seeming to confirm the theory. But, in addition to that factor, the general increase in orchid cultivation must have a lot to do with it. As a genus, paphiopedilums gained enormously in those peak decades.

A seedling will frequently make more than one growth before flowering and must be given pot room to do so.

# Seedlings and raising them

Buying flasks of seedling paphiopedilums is a rather risky procedure for anyone inexperienced in treatment of such plants. If unable to resist the temptation, it is sometimes better to take in a partner as where one fails the other may be able to make a go of it.

On taking delivery the flask should, if possible, be collected from the nursery, but it sometimes arrives by mail. There is little advantage in keeping the tiny seedlings in the flask until they grow a little larger, because once they are taken away from the conditions they were accustomed to at the nursery, they stop growing anyway unless a very fine equivalent set of conditions of light and warmth can be provided.

The best way to remove them from the flask, other than breaking it, is to fill it to about the half-way level with clean water to which a small amount of Natriphene has been added. The flask should then be gently swirled to loosen the small plants from the culture medium. Once they are loosened, they should be gently removed with a long pair of tweezers, or poured out on to a piece of cloth which will allow them to drain. When they are all out they should be graded into roughly two sizes; the largest going into one pot, the smallest into another.

The pots to take them should be prepared beforehand with a loose packing of green heads of sphagnum moss over a drainage medium, such as fine bark or any other suitable material. The moss bed should be about 2 centimetres or more deep. The small seedlings are potted into the surface of the moss, sprayed again with a weak solution of Natriphene and, pot and all, put into a plastic bag and the neck tied. This will conserve the moisture in the moss and packing material under it.

Periodically the neck of the bag should be untied and the interior sprayed with a fine spray of water, occasionally including a small amount of Natriphene. Apart from natural losses, there should be none to fungus or brown rot if the system is properly carried out.

Such flasks are not proper purchases for cold glass-house cultivation, and should preferably be bought at the beginning of the growing season.

The small plants may be potted as they develop their second or third root and benched with the other small plants in the collection.

Hot-box treatment is not usually necessary, but occasionally it helps if for some reason the root system decays and a new one must be encouraged on the tiny plants.

# Pollinating the flowers

Pollinating a paphiopedilum flower is a little more difficult than other orchid flowers. The best way to go about it is to look closely at the flower from the front and understand its construction. Immediately at the mouth of the labellum or pouch is a solid-looking plate. This is the combined pollen-carrying anthers and stigma, known as the staminode. It is quite obvious in most Slippers, pale yellow to cream colored and shaped something like a shield. On the internal upper corners of this shield the two pollinia rest. This is one of the major differences about a paphiopedilum flower compared with other orchids.

If self-pollination is the aim, the pot should be rested in a position where the back of the flower is clearly visible and open to work on. First, carefully cut away the ventral sepal, which is the lower part of the flower behind the labellum. The next step is to cut a little window in the back of the labellum so that the interior is clearly visible. (Some pollinators prefer to cut the labellum completely away, but too much mutilation of the flower could cause it to prematurely fade.) On looking into this window the back of the staminode can be seen, and it is on the rear surface that the pollen should be placed or smeared. Usually it is possible to pick the pollen off quite easily with the blunt end of a toothpick first gently rubbed on the back of the staminode to collect some of the sticky substance from the stigma.

If cross-pollination is the aim, the flower should be prepared to receive the pollen as outlined above, using a clean razor blade to make the incisions. The pollen donor is prepared in the same way if the pollinia cannot be lifted out from the front of the flower. If it can be seen and removed, there is no need to mutilate the donor flower.

Use only one of the pollen masses and it may be best to crush and smear it lightly before smearing it on the rear of the staminode, which is the stigma. The pollen is a mass of separate grains formed into a slightly glutinous nob or globule. There is no real cavity, such as in a cymbidium flower, where the pollen can be pushed in and that is the reason why it may be best to first smear or crush it.

Paphiopedilum flowers should be mature when the pollen is removed or when the flower is pollinated, a condition which may take as long as a week to reach, depending on the weather or the conditions under which the plants are grown.

There is little visual indication to convey that the pollen or the stigmatic surface is mature and receptive. Pollen is more likely to deteriorate than the stigmatic surface, and when fresh should be pale to dark honey color. Brown or dark-looking pollen is usually non-fertile because it has been infected with fungus or is too old.

Seed capsules take varying periods to mature and ripen, some never seeming to swell much at all or change. The usual indication of fertility is withering of the flower, a slight swelling of the capsule, and its erection on the stem, which should remain colored and strong. It is common for a capsule to take up to twelve months to ripen.

When the pollen is placed on the stigmatic surface and it is fertile, it grows a number, sometimes a large number, of fine, hair-like filaments down through the stigma and into the ovary, where the embryonic seeds are borne in separate rows in separate compartments. The filaments carry the sperm cells into the embryos and create fertile seeds, in the process reducing the number of chromosomes that each contributes to a half or haploid number.

In many hybrid paphiopedilums the half number may have attached what are called univalents or odd chromosomes, which confuse and frequently sterilise the clone so

*Paphio.* Hellas 'Westonbirt' was forecast as an outstanding parent by the breeder, H.G. Alexander.

that it is useless for further breeding. This may in part account for infertile and non-maturing seed capsules.

Although there has been little chromosome counting, from the appearance of the plants it could be expected that many of the Slippers carry double sets of chromosomes or are at least polyploid — they carry above the ordinary number of chromosomes.

Reference to robust appearance of these proposed polyploids is interesting in more ways than one, because in certain plants the bacteria in the cells which absorb nitrogen are much more numerous and active in polyploid members than in normal diploid plants. It is easy to translate a similar capacity to orchids and, with enhanced nitrogen absorption, the plant should naturally grow larger. This could in part account for the increase in size of certain early hybrids and their ability to pass this new hereditary characteristic on to future generations in plant form as well as flower size. It is difficult to account for the increase in the size of the foliage in any other way because, other than *Paphio. villosum,* all the species have short to moderate foliage, up to about 2 centimetres wide and 20-odd centimetres long.

# Watering

The most frequent question is, how often should orchids be watered? The simple and perhaps evasive answer to that is to water them when they need it. That is hardly good enough, but at the same time a little common sense should be expected of questioners. Slippers grow only where there is plenty of water when they need it, which is in their growing season.

In glass-house cultivation, which is the only reasonable way to grow these orchids, it is impossible to recreate anything remotely resembling their original habitat, but remember the saying that they are very much a product of their environment, even if that bears no resemblance whatever to the mountains, gullies, cliffs, trees, moss-covered rocks and associated plants and lichens and the climate from which they emerged. Instead of all that, our domesticated and inbred plants are put into 12-15 centimetre pots on average, along with perhaps a few different types of plants or orchids in a glass-house.

A climate must be created. This is accomplished with the assistance of three things — water, air and light. Each of these things affects the others. The humidity or water content of the whole glass-house remains constant only if it is replaced as air circulation, and light or warmth brought with the light takes it away. Therefore, water comes first.

Air must flow about the plants because one of the sources of food for plants like Slippers, carbon dioxide, is taken from the air by the leaves; the carbon is retained for use by the plant and the oxygen returned to the air. If air cannot flow naturally about the plants it must be induced to do so by always adjusting the ventilators so that it can flow, or helping it to flow by using a fan. The plants breathe, so that in the order of things air must be placed second on the list. When the plants are watered they should be thoroughly soaked so that the air contained in the potting material is replaced by water and as this flows away a fresh flow of air is induced in the pot. This is an ideal cycle and one of the vital things missing by transferring an epiphytic plant into a 12 or 15 centimetre pot, and it also keeps the potting material fresh and aerated.

As no plants can thrive without light, the Slippers should get sufficient but not an oversupply, which will burn the leaves. Unrealistic as it may seem, light comes only third in the scheme of things, in spite of its necessity.

There is no way these things can be separated from each other, so the first thing is to create an environment with all of them in balance. As more orchids are killed, or prevented from growing, by overwatering than from any other cause, a rule must be worked out so that the plants, while never dehydrated, are never watered until the previous watering has almost dried out of the potting material. There is very little chance that the plants will die quickly from dryness. In reducing the answer to an ultimate factor, no plant in the collection should be allowed to go dry for more than a day.

Watering, of course, is seasonally balanced. If a glass-house is internally warmed the plants will tend to dry out a little faster in certain parts of the house than others, so that while some plants will be watered once a week, others may need it more frequently. Each must be treated individually in a process which also takes into account the size of the pot in which each plant is growing.

The whole of the growing area should be kept moist to wet — the benches, the floor and the walls. If a meter is used it should read not lower than 75-80 per cent humidity.

One of the advantages of the closed bench is that it is much easier to stabilise a glass-house so fitted. A windy day and good ventilation soon dries out a glass-house with open benches, where the moist bed of filling on the closed bench will always retain its moisture.

A definite answer, instead of evasion, can only be reduced to a time period beyond which it would be foolish not to water. This could be put at a week, provided humidity is maintained in the glasshouse. So we get down to a constant of once a week, and perhaps more often if needed.

No pot which remains wet longer than the general run should be left without finding out why. Usually it is poorly drained and the plant should be repotted. Probably when it is watered the pot completely fills with water and remains so for quite a long time.

At no time should any glass-house be converted into a sealed unit, even if it is air-conditioned on a recirculating system. Ventilators should always be open fractionally.

Shading should be so arranged that it is sufficient for the brightest days of summer, even if a little dull on overcast days. The alternative is a variable system and several of these may be thought up, even to the extent of automatic operation.

In most conditions a liner of any of the tough plastic films like Visqueen could give a temperature increase in cold weather of up to three or four degrees, and will certainly assist humidity and cut heating costs.

There is not much difference in the shade needed above Slippers in summer or winter, although if the roof is painted it will wear a bit thin by early winter. The amount of renewal depends on the location of the glass-house, both in the matter of latitude south of the equator and its situation relative to other features which may shade it. The flowers, however, do need protection from direct sunlight, which quickly fades them.

All these things are related to watering, and we get back to the thoughts at the beginning of the section. How can we tell when the plants need watering? Possibly the best answer is that experience is the best teacher, sad experience or happy experience at the things we do right and those we do wrong.

The pests which infest paphiopedilums are much the same as those which infest cymbidiums and all other orchids and glass-house plants, with another which is more prevalent on Slippers, the mealy bug. It is hard to eliminate once it gets in and the usual point of entry is an infested plant brought into the glass-house from another collection, or infected potting material.

Mostly infestation by any pests is the result of neglect, therefore, if Slippers are grown as close together as they prefer, a constant watch should be kept on the underside of the leaves, because that is where scale usually attaches itself. Mealy bug also keeps well out of sight and reach of the hose.

Two forms of scale infest Slippers; the common mussel scale and the white scale, which when examined is almost the same. Both are hard to get rid of once they are allowed to come in. The usual systemic sprays should be used as a routine procedure about twice a year, the first when repotting is finished and the second about the beginning to end of March. When repotting, each plant in the glass-house should be examined by inverting it and looking carefully at the underside of the leaves. Most frequently, infected plants can be spotted by leaves which look dehydrated on the upper surface.

Bud loss is often put down to careless watering, with the buds rotting in the axils of the leaves just as they start to emerge. All too frequently the cause is a fungus infection — the same one which will rot the leaves in cold, humid conditions. It can be kept at bay with any of the dual-purpose systemic sprays. Most of these will not harm the buds if applied in March and the residue, which may give the foliage a dusty and unsightly appearance, will keep washing down into the leaf axils and adding to the protection. Some sprays used for scale and insect pests, however, will damage immature buds and such as E605 or Parathion, Lindane, Malathion and others should be used only in the growing period, and not when there is any likelihood of bud damage.

Baiting for slugs and snails should be additional to keeping the floor and benches clean and free from pots and other debris. If ferns or other plants are grown in the same glass-house, they should also be watched for scale, mealy bug and other pests. It is quite safe to use the sprays not recommended for budding Slippers to keep these plants free.

While it is possible to mix many other orchids with Slippers in a glass-house, they should preferably be types which can be suspended over the Slipper benches in positions where they will not block out too much light. It is best to keep the Slippers free from outsiders so that they may treated as a whole collection. If overhead plants are grown they should not be allowed to drip water into the leaf axils of the Slippers.

The inside of the roof should be sprayed, irrespective of the type of orchids grown. It should be done at least once a year, preferably after the roof is painted or just before winter, when more condensation forms to cause drips on to the plants.

At the first sign of brown rot this should be the first area for attention, followed by complete spraying of the plants, even if approaching flowering time.

Slippers seem to be free of virus infections; although I have heard plants condemned as having virus, I have never seen one with indications which led me to think it had this disease. At times I have been asked if a certain Slipper plant has virus and it is always a difficult question to answer. Mostly the owner seems to be looking for a

167

Fungus related diseases are the most common forms attacking Slippers and permanently disfigure the foliage.

negative answer. The plants I have seen which suggested virus infection have always been badly neglected and usually grown as one of a few Slippers in a mixed collection of orchids, and frequently attacked by brown rot. Occasionally this disease has the appearance of virus infection with brown spotting of the foliage. The real test is whether the new foliage is affected, and this is the only real visual test. If it is clean there is little to worry about.

Some orchids must be grown in isolation because the conditions they need as a genus are too insular for a mixture of genera. Two in this category are odontoglossums and phalaenopsis. Slippers are not at all like that and may be grown with other genera, although grouped for preference and not mixed. While one section is devoted to them, there is no limit to the correctly selected genera which could be grown in the remaining space.

People who grow one or two Slippers mixed in with other genera will probably miss the best these orchids can produce and should look to other orchids if they like a miscellaneous collection. The early growers of the genus perhaps had intuition to guide them, because they devoted a complete growing area to each genus. Perhaps life was not so complicated then, as most of the growers were certainly affluent.

However, it is also on record that many of the small homes in the towns and cities of England had glass-houses, however diminutive by comparative standards, where they grew orchids and other plants, and each seemed to have a speciality. Perhaps they, too, were quite happy with the culls from the large collections — at least they were orchids.

168

# Judging awards

Nearly all orchid societies have a system for awarding certificates for merit gained by various clones of orchids. Although the number of points awarded to these particular clones in gaining certificates may differ from state to state and country to country, they basically represent three grades of excellence: a Highly Commended award is usually the lowest of the group, an Award of Merit next, and a First Class Certificate the highest. While some societies and groups use a system of visual appreciation in which points are finally awarded, others have a system of giving points for certain features, such as shape, color, number of flowers and so forth. All lead to the one end — to recognise certain standards as the ultimate aim in hybridising.

Another distinct award is aimed at recognising outstanding clones for certain characteristics, the paramount of which eventually turns out to be color. It is usually termed an Award of Distinction.

It is possible for a clone to be judged more than once in the expectation that a better flowering might give it a chance of winning a higher award than the one originally recognised as its level. This has occurred many times in judging history in most countries.

Orchid societies have been successfully affiliated throughout the world in some instances and adopt common standards by which the flowers are judged. However, it is of little use detailing these standards, which may at times be varied or changed. The important thing about them is that wherever in the world a propagation of an awarded clone is grown, it is entitled to have the affix HCC, AM or FCC or the lower award of AD appended to its name, followed by the initials of the society which gave the award. Thus, to quote an instance, *Cymbidium* Pearl Balkis 'Pink Perfection', HCC, AOC, OCSA.

An explanation of that is, when a plant is given an award it should also be designated as a clone, in this instance 'Pink Perfection', which distinguishes it from all other clones of *Cymbidium* Balkis. The two societies which issued awards to this clone are the Australian Orchid Council and the Orchid Club of South Australia.

That these two societies have given this clone an HCC does not debar it from submission to judges when a higher award is sought, and this may be done anywhere else in the world; some societies may consider it worth an Award of Merit or even a First Class Certificate. It may also be resubmitted to the AOC and the OCSA, if thought appropriate. The system applies to nearly all orchids, and standards are set to be applied when orchids are submitted for judgment.

There are two other main certificates awarded: a Cultural Certificate for well grown and flowered plants, and a Certificate of Commendation, which may be considered by some as an interim recognition pending submission for a higher award perhaps on a better plant.

# Bibliography

*A Manual of Orchidaceous Plants,* James Veitch, original edition, 1887
*A Survey of the Slipper Orchids,* Waters and Waters
*Botany: An Introduction to Plant Science,* Robbins, Weier and Stocking
*Formosan Orchids,* Chow Cheng
*Indian Orchids,* Volume 1, Udai C. Pradhan
*Generic Names of Orchids,* Schultes and Pease
*Johnson's Botanical Dictionary,* 1917
*Orchids for Everyone,* Charles Curtis
*Orchids,* Lewis Castle
*Paxton's Botanical Dictionary,* 1868
'Proceedings Papers, 4th World Orchid Conference', K. C. Pradhan
*Sanders Orchid Hybrid List,* 1869-1975
*Sanders Orchid Guide,* 1927 edition
*Sertum Orchidaceum,* John Lindley, 1838
*The Orchid Album,* R. Warner and B. S. Williams
*The Orchid Review* (England), 1893-1979
*The Australian Orchid Review,* 1939-79

# Index